RESCUED
by the
Cross

ABOUT THE AUTHOR

Abused and neglected, Freeman grew up in a fatherless home with an alcoholic mother. As a child, he knew nine different stepfathers and attended twenty-four different schools. Eventually, a nightmarish home life drove him to the streets.

Drawn to a church revival by the offer of free pizza, Freeman accepted Christ at the age of sixteen. The street-hardened teenager experienced God's healing power and soon felt a desire to fulfill God's will and purpose for his life. At nineteen, Freeman joined a traveling music ministry, and at twenty-two he moved into full-time positions as minister of youth and music. His own harsh experiences and his rapport with young people ultimately led to a God-given concern for teenagers and families.

And now, after sixteen years in full-time evangelism, Ken Freeman shares his message of hope across the country and has seen more than 100,000 people accept Christ as Lord and Savior.

Freeman's family ministry blesses many through couples' retreats and family-oriented revivals.

In contrast to his horror-filled childhood, Freeman's adult home life is a miracle of God. He and his wife, Debbie, have been married twenty-five years and have two sons, Josh and Jeremy.

RESCUED by the CROSS

Stepping Out of Your Past and into God's Purpose

KEN FREEMAN
with
Ken Walker

Our purpose at Howard Publishing is to:

- *Increase faith* in the hearts of growing Christians
- *Inspire holiness* in the lives of believers
- *Instill hope* in the hearts of struggling people everywhere

Because He's coming again!

Published by Howard Publishing Co., Inc., 3117 North 7th Street, West Monroe, Louisiana 71291-2227 in association with the literary agency of Wolgemuth & Associates, Inc., 330 Franklin Rd., Ste. 135A-106, Brentwood, Tennessee 37027.

04 05 06 07 08 10 9 8 7 6 5 4

Library of Congress Cataloging-in-Publication Data
Freeman, Ken, 1952–
Rescued by the cross : stepping out of your past and into God's purpose / Ken Freeman.
p. cm.
Includes bibliographical references.
ISBN 1-58229-303-1 (pbk.)
1. Youth—Religious Life. @. Freeman, Ken, 1952– . I. Title.
BV4531.2.F73 1999
248.8′3—dc21 98-48300
CIP

Edited by Jennifer Stair
Interior design by Vanessa Bearden
Cover design by LinDee Loveland

All first names have been changed to protect the privacy of the individuals.

CONTENTS

FOREWORD

In the early 1980s our young people attended a camp that was under the leadership of Ken Freeman. I will never forget the way God used him in the lives of those young people. He had the blessed anointing of the Holy Spirit upon his life. At the same time I was surprised by his radical commitment to the Lord Jesus Christ. Quite honestly, I was not sure that Ken would make it through the long haul of ministry life.

Over the years I have seen God mature him in a very special way. He has continued to grow as a Christian. Being on the speaking circuit has never become routine for him.

To everyone who has ever been abused . . .

wounded . . .

ashamed . . .

afraid . . .

or hopeless . . .

There is hope.

Someone knows your pain.
He can rescue you from your despair.

Look to the Cross.

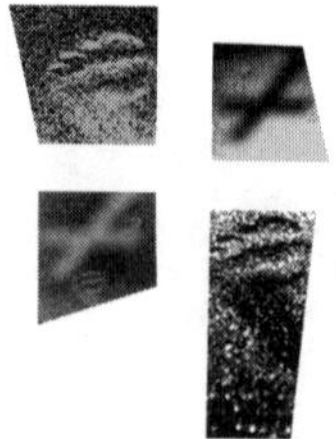

He has always had the passion to stand before God's people with a word from the Lord. Being cute or relevant has never been his ultimate goal. Even as he has matured, God still uses him in the lives of teenagers and adults.

My boys, Josh and Nick, love Ken Freeman. They love him because he is real. They love him because he is radical. They love him because he loves people. They love him because they have seen him invest his life in others.

The story of Ken Freeman that you are about to read will light your spiritual fire. His life is a great picture of God's transforming power. Ken is a radical for Jesus Christ. He is not radical simply for the sake of being radical. He is radical because God has changed his life and he has never gotten over it.

When I served as the president of the Southern Baptist Convention's Pastors Conference, I felt led of God to have Ken on the program. God used him in a powerful way. In fact, his message was the number two audiotaped message purchased out of all the preachers on that program.

Ken relates because he is real. He relates because he is refreshing. He relates because he is God's man.

Get ready. Tighten your seat belt. The journey you are about to go on through reading this book will be a thrilling adventure that will remind you that we serve an all-powerful God. No one is ever beyond his reach.

In some ways, Ken is like a John the Baptist to our generation. Let God use him and the work God has done in his life to challenge and bless you.

Enjoy the journey!

Dr. Ronnie W. Floyd
Senior Pastor
First Baptist Church
Springdale, Arkansas

WITH GRATITUDE

I would like to express my gratitude to the many people who encouraged me to share the message of healing and hope found at the cross of Jesus Christ.

First of all, I thank my Lord and Savior Jesus Christ for changing my life and dying for me on the cross.

Also, I am very grateful for my wife, Debbie, and for the journey that we have taken together. Debbie, I could never thank you enough. You're a great wife and great mom and wonderful grandma. Your love and encouragement have been my strength and support. I love you, Babe; you are the first love of my life. Thank you for always being there, caring for me, and partnering with me to share the hope of the Cross.

And to the rest of our wonderful family—Jeremy, Josh, Tammy, and Canaan (the second loves of my life)—thank you all for loving me unconditionally and lifting me up in prayer by kneeling at the Cross.

I also want to thank Debbie's mom and dad, Mr. and Mrs. Tedder, for giving me their wonderful daughter to be my wife and for being such great role models of the Cross.

I am grateful to Malcolm and Johnie Grainger, my "Jesus parents," for believing in me and showing me how to live each day in honor of the Cross.

Thanks to Jack Taylor and Castle Hills First Baptist Church for teaching me to grow in my faith and for keeping me focused on the Cross.

A special thanks to Jay Hall, Dave King, Chuck Sugar, Martin Culpepper, and all the SirReal Records family for supporting me and helping me spread the message of the Cross.

I am grateful to the family at Howard Publishing for catching the vision for this book and to Ken Walker and Jennifer Stair for helping me communicate the power of the Cross.

Thanks also to all the guys in Among Thorns for leading me in praise and worship at the foot of the Cross.

I am especially grateful to Andy Hornbaker Jr., Craig Miller, Don Babin, Dr. Ronnie Floyd, Dr. Claude Thomas, and many other ministers for

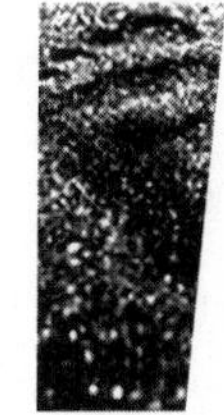

encouraging me and giving me countless opportunities to lead others to the Cross.

Thank you to David Walker, my pastor and friend, and to my church family, Alamo City Christian Fellowship, for their support, love, and prayers and for standing with me at the Cross.

Finally, I am thankful for you, the reader. As you read this book and discover how Jesus Christ changed my life, I pray that you, too, will be transformed by entrusting your life to the One who gave himself for you on the cross. As Jesus said, "I, when I am lifted up from the earth, will draw all men to myself" (John 12:32).

PART ONE

RESCUED by the Cross

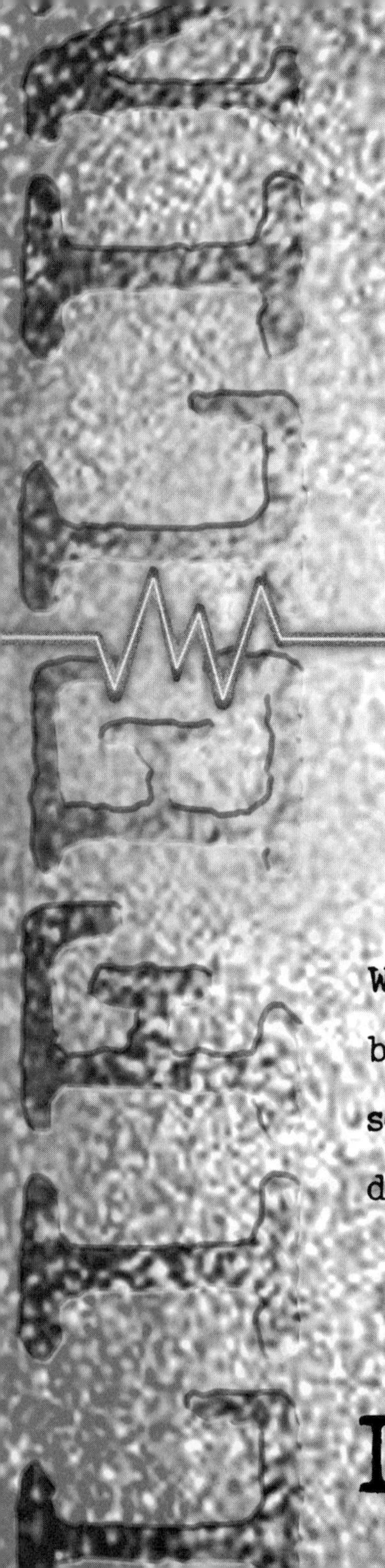

Wine makes you mean,
beer makes you quarrel-
some—a staggering
drunk is not much fun.

—Proverbs 20:1 *The Message*

LIFELINE

1 Butchered Dreams

The blade must have been a foot long. Grasping the thick wooden handle, my mother wielded the knife with a threatening swoosh as she hovered over our bunk beds. My sister, Donna, and I had awakened wide-eyed when she stumbled into our bedroom. The sickening, stale odor of alcohol lingered in the air.

"You were a mistake," she declared in a menacing tone. The darkness hid her face from me. "A very costly mistake. You've cost me way too much money. And for what? You're worthless, you know that? You came from hell. You'll never go anywhere. You'll never amount to anything—just like your worthless father."

"Mommy, what's wrong?" I asked, trembling.

"I'm tired of living," she mumbled, looking over my shoulder as if she were talking to the wall. She paused. I stared at the knife, each second a heart-pounding test of my will to survive. At nine years old, I had already experienced enough physical abuse and emotional trauma to last a lifetime. Would this night be the end of my tortured life?

"I'll kill you both," she sneered after staring into space for what seemed like an eternity. "Then I'll kill myself."

"No, Mommy, no!" I pleaded. "Stop! Please! Don't do it! Please, Mommy! Don't hurt us!"

"I'll kill you both," she sneered. "Then I'll kill myself."

A flood of tears poured from my eyes. My cries soon escalated into hysterical sobs and screams, which sent Donna into spasms. I couldn't understand her indecipherable babbling, but I remember Donna's shoulders heaving as she shook her head back and forth. The sight of us wailing and begging for mercy must have snapped Mom out of her liquor-stained haze. She sank slowly onto the edge of the bed and began to cry. The knife slid from her grasp.

"It's all right," Mom choked. "I'm not going to kill you. I was just a little upset."

My heart pounding, I lay in my bed for hours,

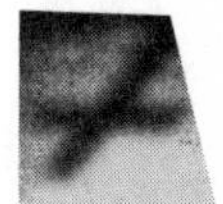

unable to sleep. As I stared at the dark ceiling, I wondered why my mother was so angry. She had been born in South Carolina to hard-working, church-going parents. She told me they never drank, smoked, or cussed. A straight-A student through the eighth grade, my mother took her first drink at a party when she was fifteen. That one drink apparently touched off her love affair with booze.

Her alcoholism drove her to wander chaotically from place to place. Living first near the East Coast, she wandered to California where she met and married her second husband (my father), who was serving in the navy. Then she drifted back east and on into the Midwest. I was born in Virginia; two years later my sister arrived while we were living in Kansas City, Missouri. During my childhood we roamed through North Carolina, South Carolina, Tennessee, Kansas, Illinois, Arkansas, Washington, Michigan, Texas, and several other states. Our longest stay in one place was in the Saint Louis area. Even there we bounced around like pinballs, moving from suburb to suburb.

I never understood why my mother grew to hate my father with such a passion. They met when he was in the navy. Both of them were heavy drinkers, which marred their hopes of a long and happy marriage. Deep wounds inflicted by her miscarriage of twins a year before my birth were salved with more alcohol. But booze didn't cure my mother's pain; it only numbed her for a few hours.

I was only four when my parents divorced. Though my father initially secured visitation rights, Mom pumped us so full of her venom toward Dad that we complained and asked embarrassing questions whenever we visited him. Finally he put his foot down, telling my mother, "Either you take full custody of them, or I'll take full custody. I'm tired of dragging these kids back and forth between the two of us." We never went back to Dad's house.

THE ABUSE BEGINS

The end of our visits to Dad didn't bring Mom much satisfaction. Though she occasionally smiled and even laughed, these brief moments of normalcy didn't make up for her frequent dark moods. I was barely five years old when the abuse began, intensifying as we grew older. She regularly cursed at us and frequently beat us or banished us to our bedroom. Her fearsome eruptions were capped off by screaming commands. Donna and I never knew what to expect from Mom. We might come home after a pleasant day at school, only to be

I was barely five years old when the abuse began.

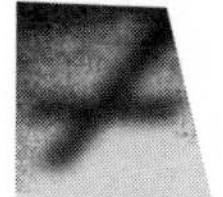

greeted by flying fists, a dinner plate sailing through the air, or a stream of profanity that punctured our spirits like a dagger.

But Mom's physical and verbal attacks were not our only problems. A recurring pattern of neglect left us frightened and confused. She would vanish for several days at a time, wedging toothpicks in the front door and warning that any broken pieces would alert her that we had left without her permission. It never dawned on us that, with her thinking clouded by liquor, she would forget leaving them there.

A steady stream of parties passed through whatever place we called home for the moment. Even in the rare times when nobody drifted by for a snort, Mom's fingers would be curled around a shot glass filled with amber-colored liquid. After emptying it, she would take a swig from a glass of water, which sat next to an ashtray that held burning cigarettes around the clock. Her eyes were continually bloodshot.

While somewhat stable during the week, on Fridays she would often disappear, leaving us with whatever bar buddy she could sweet talk into babysitting her little "brats." Sometimes her flings would move in for a while, compensating themselves for their services by dipping into Mom's

stash of liquor. Most of these baby-sitters weren't dependable, dashing out the door moments after Mom left us in their care. Our temporary guardians included ex-boyfriends or new lovers whom she lured to the task with the promise of sex or other favors. The latter led to one of the most humiliating incidents of our lives.

This traumatic event occurred the first night an ex-boyfriend stayed with us while Mom took off for three days of drinking and waiting on tavern customers. I remember crawling up the ladder into the top bunk, laughing, and making playful remarks to Donna before we drifted off to sleep. I awoke to terrible noises. Looking down, I saw our baby-sitter on top of Donna, but at seven years old, I had no idea what he was doing. Scared and unsure of what was happening, I pretended to be asleep. But after she screamed twice, I yelled at him. I had already learned how to cuss, so I used a few choice words.

Since he had finished raping Donna, he reached up and pulled down my pants. Though he didn't rape me, I don't remember much about the molestation; I think my mind has blocked out the trauma. But I do remember having to spend two more days with him until Mom returned.

When I finally told Mom what had happened,

she went crazy. I'm not sure who she called, but the police showed up and asked me a string of questions. Later they returned and took me to the police station, where a cop hoisted me up so I could see through the lockup window. I pointed out the attacker, but he never looked up. Later I had to repeat the experience in a courtroom. Fortunately, the lawyers didn't ask too many questions. I swore to tell the truth, pointed at the defendant, and said he was the one who had done those terrible things to my sister and me. We never saw him again.

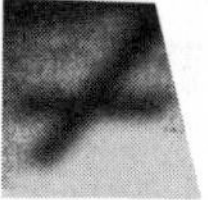

Still traumatized from the molestation and angry at the wild whippings from my new stepfather, I tried to commit suicide two years later, when I was only nine. Before going to bed I managed to sneak a bottle of aspirin out of the kitchen and swallow all of its contents. I had seen someone do that in a movie and thought it would take care of my problems. Going to sleep and never waking up seemed much better than living. I'm not sure that I really wanted to die; I just wanted the pain to stop.

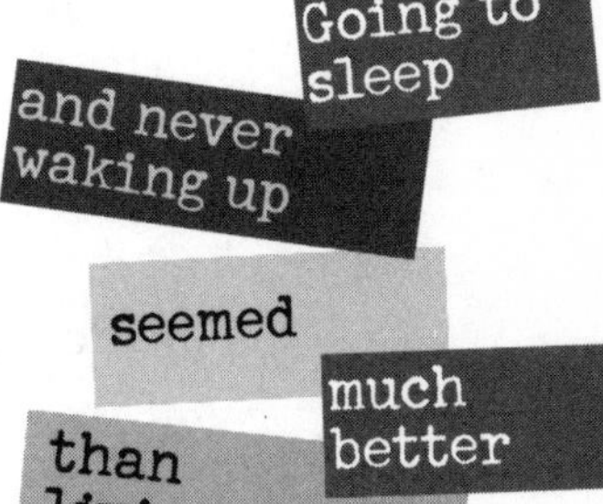

Living in Denial

Those who think booze is harmless seldom acknowledge the squalor, wasted lives, and broken homes left in

alcohol's bitter wake. And they do not like to hear the truth that countless parents haul their children into bars. As a boy I spent hundreds of hours in smoke-filled taverns. Donna and I would play shuffleboard and pool while my mother and her partner downed another drink.

Depictions of harmless, fun-loving, tipsy drunks have long been a staple of American cartoons, movies, and television shows. Such humorous characterizations reflect society's ingrained philosophy that overindulging in alcohol is a carefree way to have a good time. But after witnessing my mother's violent behavior whenever she was drunk, I know there is no such thing as "harmless drinking."

Citizens in the United States live in constant denial of the seriousness of the damage caused by this harmful drug. Alcohol is the leading cause of domestic violence and highway deaths—approximately three hundred thousand between 1982 and 1995, more than five times the number of Americans who died in the Vietnam War. The estimated social costs of addictions to alcohol, cigarettes, and other drugs exceed 240 billion dollars a year.[1] A recent study projects that by the year 2010 the combined costs of depression and alcohol dependency will outrank cancer as the worst burdens on America's health-care system.[2]

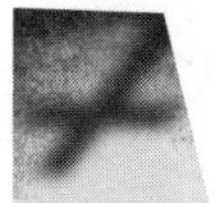

Over the years I have heard too many stories of people whose descent into despair, further drug abuse, prison time, or unwanted pregnancies originated with their first drink. If more people would have spoken out against booze, maybe my mother wouldn't have taken her first sip at age fifteen. That seemingly harmless act not only destroyed my childhood but ultimately led to her premature death at age fifty-two. That one sip also made those intervening thirty-seven years a time of misery for her and for those closest to her.

Fight to Survive

"Hey, mister. Can ya spare a quarter? Gotta make a couple of calls."

The man had just stumbled out of one of the dozens of taverns that covered our suburban, blue-collar neighborhood. Every few blocks sat a pool hall, lounge, or beer garden—usually next to a convenience store that dispensed additional beverages. If barflies didn't get enough inside, they could carry more home.

He looked over his shoulder and blinked a couple of times. Though I tried to look innocent, my faded jeans, grubby T-shirt, wiry frame, and hardened countenance labeled me a twelve-year-old hustler out to support my favorite habit. But my

request was innocent enough this night: I hoped to gather enough spare change for a couple of burgers and cokes for Donna and myself.

"Uh, yeah," he nodded slowly, fumbling in his pockets before fishing out a couple of dimes and a quarter. A beer-stained odor colored the air as he leaned over. "Here, kid. Enjoy yourself."

"Thanks, mister," I nodded, trying to project the cool manner that helped me survive on America's streets in the sixties. "I 'preciate it."

"Got enough, Ken?" Donna asked as the man hobbled down the street, muttering to himself.

"Think so. Let's check out the grill."

Scoffers may joke about "greasy spoons," but those modest diners were the highlight of our childhood. Donna and I wolfed down our burgers with as much joy as if Mrs. Cleaver had placed them gently onto our plates in a scene from *Leave It to Beaver.* Our mother rarely served a home-cooked meal: her idea of cooking dinner was plopping a box of carry-out food onto the kitchen table.

The house in Saint Louis where we were living the night we panhandled for our dinner was the closest we had ever come to a real home. The single-story frame dwelling was nothing fancy: the living room measured about twelve-by-ten feet and contained a nondescript couch, two chairs, and an old

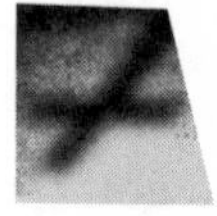

television set. The house also contained a pair of sparsely furnished bedrooms and a tiny strip of a kitchen with a small table. Donna and I slept in one of the bedrooms in sagging bunk beds—that is, when we could sleep amid the drunken, profanity-laced revelry that continued late into the night.

We never knew when Mom would burst through the door in an unexplainable rage, grab a broom, and whack our legs with the handle. After we burst into tears, she wouldn't let us go to bed until we stopped crying. We often slept by the front door so we could hear her drive up, and then we'd hide downstairs or in a neighbor's backyard until she passed out.

Since we never knew when Mom would erupt in another tirade, Donna and I spent many hours in the basement. In this safe place away from Mom, we often tossed around a rubber ball, sometimes grabbing a mop handle and pretending we were playing stickball in the alley of our neighborhood. But we mainly liked staying out of Mom's reach. She couldn't maneuver the stairs very well and usually forgot we were there. Donna and I would play until Mom left for work, then we'd watch television or roam around the neighborhood.

We never knew when Mom would erupt in another tirade.

We never had to worry about returning at a particular time since Mom usually stayed out past midnight. After our impromptu burger feast that evening, we wandered through the streets like a pair of juvenile hobos. Passing most of the time under the streetlights, we also loitered at the homes of a couple of friends whose parents lived similar lifestyles. Donna and I finally drifted home, hoping to avoid another beating.

"What's that smell?"

Donna wrinkled her nose as we slipped through the front door after midnight. Mom had arrived home first. Crumpled on the floor and lying on her side, she was clad in dingy shorts and a worn blouse. She was sleeping soundly next to a pool of drying vomit and an empty whiskey bottle. In the shadows cast by the dim streetlight, we could see two strangers sprawled on the couch, snores bubbling up from their drunken bodies.

Suddenly a surge of hatred pulsed through my veins. I impulsively walked into the kitchen and grabbed the butcher knife lying on the counter—the same one she had held over my head three years before.

Thoughts of revenge filled my mind as I dangled the blade over my mother's body. How I wanted to

Thoughts of revenge filled my mind as I dangled the blade over my mother's body.

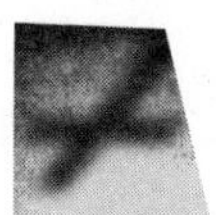

strike back at her for all the wounds she had inflicted on me! I slowly moved the knife up and down my mother's lifeless frame, starting at her stomach and grazing it along her torso until I stopped at her neck. Finally I pointed it at her face and pictured myself slashing it across her throat.

To my youthful mind, it was a game. I could pretend to attack her and get even for all the insults and injuries, and she couldn't do anything about it because she was asleep. *Take that, Mom! How does it feel to be on the other end for once? Are you scared? Are you sorry for all the times you hurt us? What did we ever do to you to deserve this? Huh? C'mon. Speak up. I've got the knife right here in my hands. You'd better be scared. This could be your time.*

Strangely, this vengeful daydream didn't bring me any satisfaction. I was overcome by emotion and began to cry. Soon my whole body was trembling.

"Do it!" Donna urged from between her teeth, which she had clenched to stifle her sobs. "Go ahead! Do it!"

I paused for a moment, still holding the knife over my mother's still body. I had the motive and enough hatred inside to finish the task. I was tough too. I had become so hardened by years of abuse that by now I could take Mom's fist to my mouth without crying.

For protection, I had developed a shell that enabled me to hide as easily as the Invisible Man. But this night exposed raw feelings and years of pent-up emotion. To this day I don't know what stopped me from using the butcher knife. Maybe my tears relieved the stress. Whatever the reason, I'm glad I stopped. Living with the guilt of murder would have created a lifetime prison, one that would have outlived temporary confinement behind bars. Despite what my mother had done, I realized that I didn't have the right to take her life. No matter how badly she had hurt me, retaliation wouldn't solve a thing. Even the temporary satisfaction of hurting the person who had hurt me so deeply couldn't reclaim my lost childhood, wipe out bitter memories, or force my mother to become responsible.

When the tears stopped and my body quit twitching, I shook my head and slowly stood up. Walking into the kitchen, I flung the knife on the counter.

"C'mon," I said to Donna. "Let's go to bed."

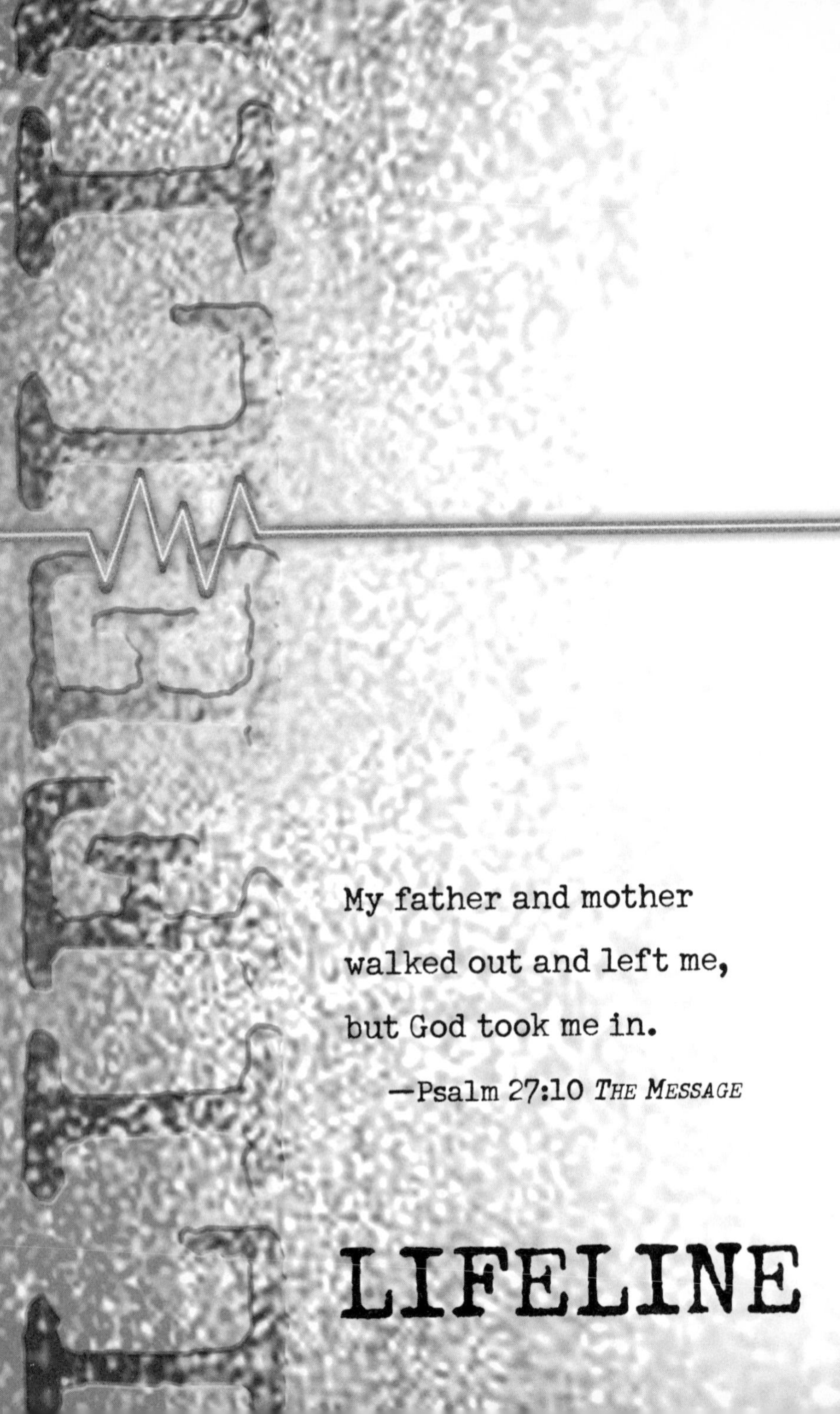

My father and mother
walked out and left me,
but God took me in.

—Psalm 27:10 *The Message*

LIFELINE

2 Broken Homes

None of the stepfathers and strangers who meandered through my life filled the simple need I had for a father. I needed someone who would teach me how to throw a ball, play catch with me, take me fishing, show me how to build a campfire, read me a bedtime story, and reassure me with a hug. I needed a father to show affection for my mother so I could know the security of a stable, loving home. I needed someone who would work hard so I could have adequate physical nourishment and provision. Most importantly, I needed a father to demonstrate responsibility so I would know how to act like a man.

I didn't have any of those things from my father. I don't know exactly when he left: One day I just realized he was gone. When I asked Mom where Dad was, she growled, "He's gone and he ain't comin' back." Oh, how I missed Dad! None of my nine stepfathers could fill the void—not even the stepfather who stayed around the longest. He tried to be a father to me. He did his best to teach me to fish, and we puttered around occasionally in the yard. He showed me how to use a lawn mower and how to tighten some nuts and bolts under the hood of his car. I appreciated those times, but I longed to have my own father as a constant part of my childhood.

This stepfather even played a little baseball with me, although I was usually such an emotional bundle of nerves that I struggled to enjoy it. I placed intense pressure on myself to perform. I thought if I did well, others would like me and want to be my friends. I managed to make a Little League team one summer, but I will never forget the day when the pressure of our dysfunctional home suddenly caved in on me. Standing in the outfield one afternoon, I dropped to the ground and dis-

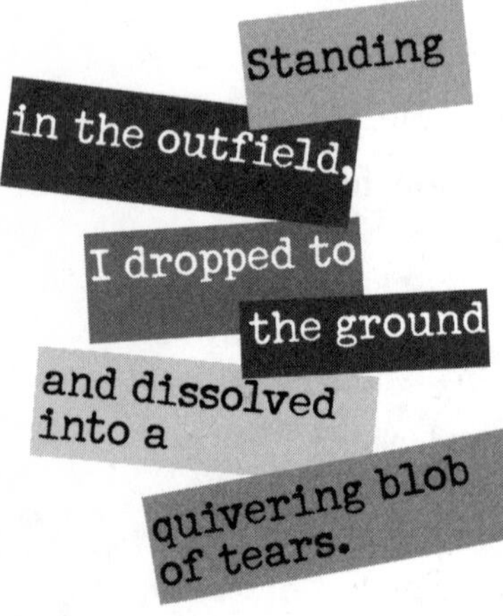

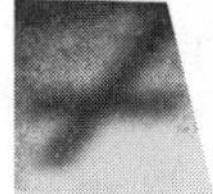

solved into a quivering blob of tears. The coach finally walked out, picked me up, and carried me back to the bench.

For years I thought all men were idiots and worthless drunks. The only male role models I knew were shiftless, dishonest vagabonds whose primary joy in life was winning a poker hand. Though I detested these men, I became just like them. Taking up smoking and drinking at the age of ten, I learned how to lie, cheat, and steal with the skill of a seasoned, small-time jailbird.

This kind of influence stirred an inward anger that fueled my disrespect for all rules and my contempt for everyone in authority. I hated my father because he wasn't around. And I hated the other men who drifted in and out of our lives—a fluctuating assortment of stepfathers, bar buddies, and other ne'er-do-wells. After my parents divorced, every man Mom married was someone she met in a tavern. I don't know if any of them ever held steady jobs because they usually walked around with hangovers. I greeted each new stepfather with hope, but it didn't take long before I despised each one of them. Instead of doing anything for us or helping Mom, they only made life worse. Instead of one drunk parent at home, now there were two, which doubled the intensity of fighting and swearing.

My worst stepfather was a whiny little guy who was even shorter than I was. And he was slower too, which meant I could outrun him whenever I made him mad. He cursed a lot and often bubbled over in tears when he got drunk. He worked as a waiter at whatever restaurant or tavern hadn't yet fired him, and he stashed whiskey in the glove compartment of his car so he didn't have to wait to get home for a snort.

I learned to drive at thirteen because of my parents' irresponsible behavior. We were on our way home one night when one of my stepfathers suddenly slumped over the wheel. Reaching from the backseat, I frantically shook him by the shoulder. Startled, he smacked the brakes and jerked the car off to the side of the road. I tried to remain calm, but the sight of him throwing up out one window while Mom vomited out the other unnerved me. Finally, he got out of the door, stumbled, and fell on the pavement. After wavering to his feet, he climbed into the backseat. I crawled up front and drove us home, my hands shaking as I strained to see over the wheel.

Father Hunger

All this happened in the fifties and sixties, that supposedly blissful era that spawned such feel-

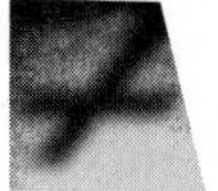

good television shows as *Leave It to Beaver, Father Knows Best, Dennis the Menace,* and *The Andy Griffith Show.* To this day I love watching the reruns, especially of Andy Griffith. Andy was a great father and Opie always called him "Pa." Andy represented the father I wanted so badly.

Occasionally I hung out with friends whose fathers lived at home. I imagined how great it would be to have a dad who came home in a good mood and spent time with his family. But most of the time I just watched television—one of our main pastimes when Mom disappeared—and daydreamed about a real family. This reverie provided a tidbit of imaginary security. Blocking out reality, I would muster enough strength to make it through another day, hoping that someday I would lead a normal life.

Despite Hollywood's images, I can't say the fifties or sixties were much fun. Nor were they very enjoyable for literally hundreds of kids I met back then. Family struggles like ours never attracted much attention. No churches, social agencies, or schoolteachers offered us a hand, though many were aware of the horrible conditions burdening us. Today's social critics make it sound as if sexual immorality, abuse, and irresponsibility suddenly blossomed in the past decade. These problems may have risen to new heights, but much of what goes on in society today also went on in the fifties.

Back then few people openly discussed dysfunctional families. From what I can remember, most people I knew treated odd behavior as normal. Since I got beat up regularly, I thought everyone slapped their kids around. I met so many other children in bars that I thought that was part of normal life too. I knew dozens of guys who didn't have fathers at home.

Despite our often-hypocritical remembrances of life in the past, we do have a serious problem today. The seeds of society's family breakdown that were planted forty and fifty years ago are now bearing rotten fruit. The father hunger that affected my life is becoming so common that, if the trend continues, society will be divided into the "haves" and "have-nots," based on whether children have a father at home. The "haves" will be the lucky few kids whose fathers decided to stick around; the "have-nots" will be those whose fathers were merely sperm donors.

Since I got beat up regularly, I thought everyone slapped their kids around.

In his book, *Fatherless America,* David Blankenhorn outlines a gloomy picture of the fatherlessness that threatens the future of our nation. In 1960,

more than 82 percent of children lived with their father. Thirty years later that figure had dropped by more than 20 percent. The percentage of those under eighteen who lived apart from their fathers in 1990 translated into a frightening number: nearly sixty-four million.[1] That is an army of children growing up without the discipline, stability, guidance, and resolve provided by a good father. Not surprisingly, 70 percent of all juveniles in state reform institutions come from fatherless homes.[2]

Equally frightening are projections for the future if the rates of divorce and illegitimacy continue their present course. Two Harvard University professors have estimated that 60 percent of children born during the nineties will end up living in single-parent homes. This bleak picture led Blankenhorn to declare fatherlessness the most harmful demographic trend of this generation:

> [Fatherlessness] is the leading cause of declining child well-being in our society. It is also the engine driving our most urgent social problems, from crime to adolescent pregnancy to child sexual abuse to domestic violence against women. Yet, despite its scale and social consequences, fatherlessness is a problem that is frequently ignored

> or denied. Especially within our elite discourse, it remains a problem with no name. If this trend continues, fatherlessness is likely to change the shape of our society.[3]

As Blankenhorn points out, we are already reaping some of the awful consequences of the absence of fathers. I believe one reason young women become sexually active is they are missing out on a daddy's love. They are looking for a boyfriend who can play that role, so they give in to having sex to gain his acceptance. Many guys are also searching for the love that is missing in their homes. Deprived of a father who can show them what it means to treat a woman with care and respect, they substitute physical pleasure for the emotional fulfillment they crave.

There are no easy answers for reversing this awful trend. Yet we clearly must regain respect for fatherhood and the institution of marriage if we want to reduce the number of children growing up without two stable parents in the same home. During the last fifty years, our standards and values have fizzled away. Too many couples today don't look at marriage as a "till death do us part" proposition. They treat what should be an enduring relationship as a matter of convenience. They are faithful as long as it suits their whims. At the first

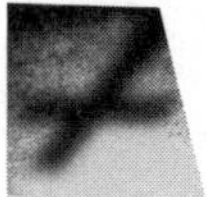

sign of trouble they're likely to shrug, "Oh well, we made a mistake. Let's just get a divorce."

Of course, not every marriage that stays together deserves to be praised. Children can live at home with both parents and still grow up without a father. When a father is always at the office or on the golf course, he has in essence abandoned his children. A father who is never home or doesn't pay any attention to his children may as well not exist. I have counseled dozens of young men and women who resent their fathers—not because their fathers physically deserted the family, but because they were so emotionally distant that their children never developed any kind of real relationship with them.

Too many men think that if they bring home enough money to feed their family, put clothes on their backs, and send the kids to school, they have fulfilled their responsibility as a father. Not true! Putting in forty hours a week to earn a salary is just the beginning. A father's job at home goes far beyond lounging in the recliner and holding the remote control. Once a man has provided for his family's physical needs, he still has obligations to spend quality time with his children, meeting their emotional needs for security, acceptance, and love.

Even beyond meeting his family's physical and

emotional needs, a father has spiritual obligations. I don't mean that every man must be a pastor or great spiritual teacher. But a good father needs to lead family devotions. His children need to see him reading the Bible and praying every day. He should take his family to church, not merely send them. Children need to know that their earthly father must rely on his heavenly Father for wisdom and strength.

But in our hectic, fast-paced society, fathers often don't spend the kind of quality time with their children that is needed to develop a strong relationship. With more and more families relying on two incomes for survival, many young people I meet share similar descriptions of a frenzied home life.

Mom, Dad, and two children dash around the house in the morning as they get ready to head off in separate directions. They don't sit down for breakfast as a family; they just grab a piece of toast before flying out the door.

After school, the boy has football practice, and the girl goes to cheerleading. Both stop afterward for a fast-food snack or at a friend's house for dinner.

Mom comes home to an empty house and fixes herself a meal as she watches the evening news alone. Dad is working late at the office, where he will order a takeout dinner to munch on at his desk.

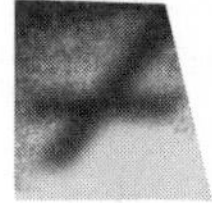

Though the children get home early enough to spend time with Mom, they quickly retreat to their bedrooms to watch television, talk on the phone, or cruise the Internet.

Dad gets home so late that all he can do is wave to the kids before they fall asleep. He and his wife don't talk much either; they are too exhausted.

In the morning, this family will arise to repeat this hurried schedule, rarely spending any meaningful time together. Living in the same house and sharing the same lives, these family members are so emotionally distant that they may as well be living in different cities. Since families like this are very common these days, it's no wonder that even children who are fortunate enough to have a father living in the same house still feel as if they are fatherless.

We must project a message of hope to those who have suffered from fatherlessness, either from physical desertion or emotional distance. Millions of young adults need to know that childhood abuse and neglect don't have to condemn them to a life of misery. Not every dysfunctional home is a failure; many children rise above adversity and go on to see their dreams come true. For example, the lack of a solid father figure ultimately helped me become a

There are no perfect fathers, only human ones.

better father. After turning my life around, I met the woman who has been my wife for more than twenty-five years. We have two fantastic sons and a grandson whom I love dearly.

Sure, I made mistakes—lots of them. There are no perfect fathers, only human ones. But my childhood neglect made me determined to be loving and sensitive to our sons' needs. I tried to give them the time, attention, and security I lacked. I wanted to be the kind of father who came to their ball games, took them on vacations, and made them proud to proclaim, "That's my dad."

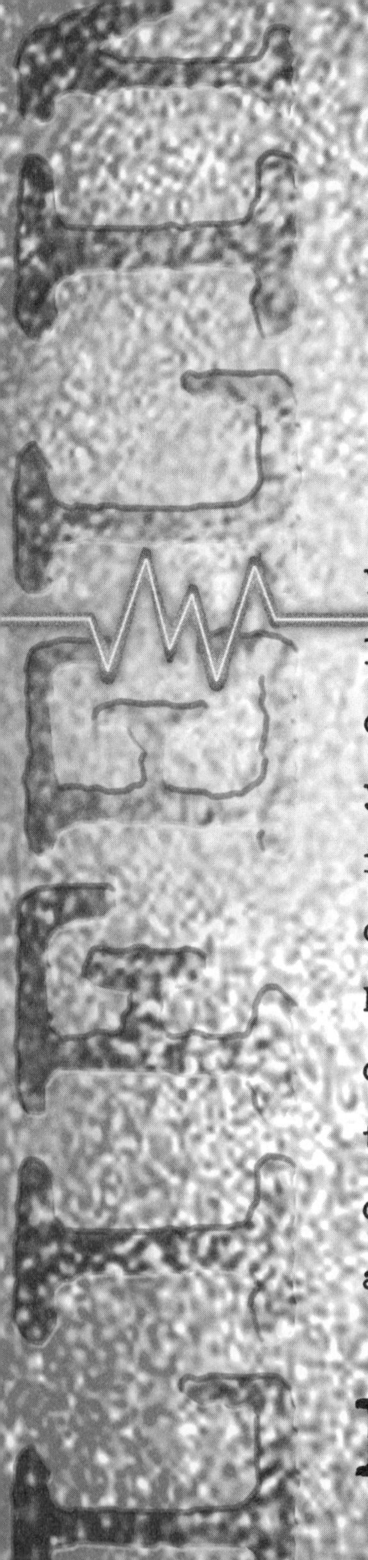

You're done with that old life. It's like a filthy set of ill-fitting clothes you've stripped off and put in the fire. Now you're dressed in a new wardrobe. Every item of your new way of life is custom-made by the Creator, with his label on it. All the old fashions are now obsolete.

—Colossians 3:9-10 *The Message*

LIFELINE

3 Brand-New Life

"Hey, Ken, you awake?"

My friend looked over the back of the seat. I rubbed my eyes. Stretching and yawning, I shook my head tenderly. *Man. I had way too much to drink last night. What day is it? And where are we?*

"Yeah. But it may take me all day to get over last night," I said, swirling my tongue around my mouth. The aftereffects of booze and cigarettes tasted horrid. I imagined that a blast of my breath could kill an innocent bystander. Fortunately, my buddy hadn't tried to drive home after our night of partying. We had slept in his car in a downtown parking lot, which turned out to be across the street from a church.

"Hey, sit up," he gestured. "Look over there. There's some folks in their Sunday best. And they're spittin' nails at each other. Man, are they hot!"

"What's going on?" I asked, pushing myself up to peer out the window.

"I don't know, but they don't look very happy," he said. "They're arguing somethin' fierce. Wonder what they're so mad about? The way they're carryin' on, they might as well turn around and go back home."

"Hey, what'd ya expect?" I said, waving my hand in the air. "Bunch of hypocrites. Talking about love and fighting like cats and dogs. Church—what a joke."

Nobody had ever talked to me about God or Jesus Christ. In my opinion, church was nothing but a money-making racket.

This wasn't the first time I stayed out all night after getting drunk with friends on Saturday and awoke next to a church. We always thought it was hilarious to watch people as they walked inside. Not all of them were fighting, but enough fussed at each other or carried on that it made a good show. Nobody had ever talked to me about God or Jesus Christ. In my opinion, church was nothing but a money-making racket. I formed that opinion by occasionally watching television evangelists, who seemed to

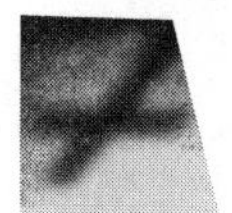

concentrate on two issues: grandiose displays of healing and urgent requests for money. *What do I need church for?* I thought after watching some slick-haired preacher beg for cash. *I can steal money.*

When I was fourteen, I had moved to Corpus Christi, Texas, with a stepfather. When this stepfather decided he had had enough of my mother, he filed for divorce and found another job. He asked if I wanted to join him after he got settled. After spending many nights sleeping in bars or other dives to avoid going home, I figured a change of scenery would do me some good. I also wanted to look out for my two younger half brothers.

Unfortunately, by the time I arrived in Corpus, my stepfather had married a woman with two of her own children. While not as abusive as my mother, she also liked liquor and inflicted some of the same physical and emotional abuse on my younger brothers. (She left me alone because I was bigger.) It didn't take long for me to figure out that the best choice was avoiding home. After school, I wasted time hanging out at the beach, the bowling alley, or bars that admitted underage drinkers. After meeting some guys who had their own cars, I got into more trouble. Whether defacing buildings, stealing, or drinking, we routinely engaged in some form of mischief.

Because my mother had moved us around so often, Corpus Christi was the first place where I spent more than one year in the same school system. I even signed up for choir—primarily because it looked like an easy credit. However, I grew to enjoy singing and made some good friends in the group. It was there I met Jeff, the person who helped me see there was a better way to live.

Invading the Enemy's Camp

Jeff McGowan was a defensive lineman on the high-school football team. We called him Cowboy because he wasn't afraid of anything or anybody—even though at six feet tall and less than two hundred pounds, he wasn't all that big. And he wasn't conceited over his status as a football star. Everyone liked Jeff, who was president of the Christian club at school. Like me, he came from a broken home, but he didn't seem soured by his past. That impressed me. He had a beautiful way of relating to other people. I wanted to be more like Jeff, but I just didn't know how.

A member of the Second Baptist Church, Jeff kept inviting me to visit. Each time, I invented a creative excuse not to go. After several rejections, Jeff told me that an evangelist named Freddie Gage was coming to his church. To persuade me to come,

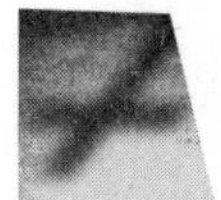

he mentioned that they were serving pizza and that some of the girls I liked would be there. As usual, I made a lame excuse.

To my surprise, Jeff showed up at my front door later that day with a firm look on his face.

"Dude, you're goin'," he proclaimed.

I thought a moment. He was bigger than I was. I didn't mind getting some free pizza. It was a chance to meet a few babes.

"Okay," I nodded.

As we drove downtown to the church, I plotted my escape. As soon as I had a chance to eat, I would sneak out the back door. When we arrived, I felt a twinge of nervousness. The only time I had been inside a church before was to steal something or to set wastebaskets on fire. I didn't really know anything about God, but I still felt spooked, wondering if my former pranks would come back to haunt me. I felt like an invader in the enemy's camp.

In spite of my cigarette-soaked, repulsive-smelling clothing, nobody shunned me.

In spite of my cigarette-soaked, repulsive-smelling clothing, nobody shunned me. I was pleasantly surprised by the people's friendliness but not by the discovery that my plans were quickly falling apart. First, I found out the pizza would be served after the service. And Jeff

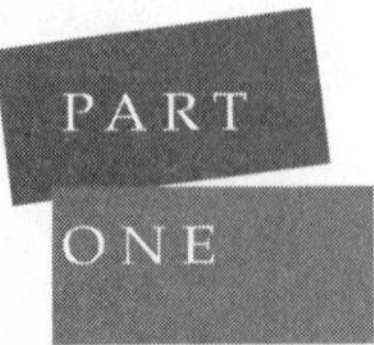

didn't intend to give me a chance to dart out early. He followed me around like a hawk before suggesting we go inside the sanctuary and find a seat. *All right,* I told myself, *I'll get through this, meet some people, and then never do this thing again.*

I wanted to sit in the back, where I could hide and maybe slip out when Jeff wasn't looking. However, I learned that if you want to get a back-row seat at church, you have to come early. I followed Jeff as he walked up to the front, onto the stage, and into the choir section! At first, I thought it was a joke. But everyone in the choir hugged me and treated me like an old friend. Soon the music started, transforming me into a choir member. I sang some familiar hymns, such as "Amazing Grace." When I didn't know a song, I stuck my head behind the book or mouthed the words silently until I picked up the tune.

When the music stopped, I analyzed the situation. Looking down at the bottom of the first page of the hymnal and seeing that the song had been written in 1732, I almost burst into laughter. I thought it was "Golden Oldies" night. This was the hippie era, and I was into the music of the Beatles, the Rolling Stones, The Who, Jefferson Airplane, and such singers as Janis Joplin, Jimi Hendrix, and

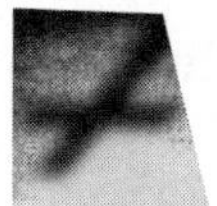

Joe Cocker. These oddballs were singing songs nearly 250 years old!

The music wasn't the only thing I found amusing. When it started and the director stood up, dramatically waving his arms, I thought he was having back spasms. These folks were definitely weird. Especially those who hugged me and said, "We love you, brother." *I don't even know who your mom is,* I thought, *so how did I become your brother?* When the evangelist came onstage, he looked like the stereotypical television preachers who I thought were all crooks. Less than six feet tall, he wore a three-piece suit with a fancy handkerchief stuck in his suit pocket and had slicked-down hair that he combed straight back. I thought this little dude was crazy before he even said a word.

To top it off, he started by telling us we were going to hell. I couldn't believe it. I thought, *I came for free food and don't even want to be in this service—and now I'm going to hell?* The nerve of that guy! I figured since I was going to hell, I should be out partying instead of listening to this guy. Before his sermon they had passed the offering plate, saying they were taking up a love offering to give to Brother Gage. I didn't give anything. Now I was really ticked off. *We just gave this guy money to yell at*

us, I fumed. *I hope they pass that plate around again because I'm going to take some money out of it.*

Listen Up

At first I didn't take Freddie Gage seriously, despite his dramatic opening line: "All my friends are dead." Gage went on to describe how he grew up on the streets of Houston, abusing drugs and running with a gang. Because he had turned his life over to God, he said, he was the only member who had survived to age twenty-five. After God turned his life around, Gage had gone back to the bars and beer joints. He now stood on pool tables to preach, warning the drunks to repent or die in their sin.

"Some of you here have been drinking," he said, a remark that startled me. *How did he know what I'd been doing?* "Some of you have done drugs and are messing up your life. I want you to know that Jesus is the only way to heaven—without him you're going to hell."

Well, I may have been on my way to hell, but at that moment I was so angry that I felt as if I had already arrived. I wanted to go up on stage, slap that evangelist around, and let him know I wasn't going to take this insult lightly. I thought Jeff had somehow slipped out before the service and told the evangelist all about me before he went on stage.

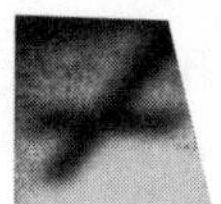

Now he was spilling my secrets to the whole church without letting the audience know he was talking about me.

Before I could act on my impulses, though, the congregation got me laughing again, shouting "Amen!" when he repeated that many of us were going to hell. *Well, he's condemning me and they think it's cool,* I chuckled. *These people are nuts.* "But some of you have been sanctified," he yelled, which provoked another chorus of "Amens" and left me scratching my head. *Sancti-what?* "Some of you have been justified," he smiled, which got a few more folks shouting and others raising their hands. I just sat there, trying to understand this funny language.

After a few more strange terms, he said, "Some of you have been convicted." So I raised my hand. I had been in a fair share of trouble with the law. I had seen jail bars from the wrong side, so I assumed you could say I had been convicted. When I glanced around and saw mine was the only hand up in the choir, I jerked it back down. *Oh, brother,* I thought, *now everybody knows I'm going to hell 'cause I've been convicted.*

Gage took a hard line toward wrongdoing, and I didn't detect much compassion in the way he preached. Yet as he talked, I could see that he really believed what he was saying. The intensity reflected in his eyes looked as if it might strike a pew and set it on fire. I was angry at his insults and suspicious of what he was saying. Still, if someone was this serious about God and could believe in him that strongly, maybe I should listen. I quit thinking about the petty things that had distracted me and started paying attention to this fiery evangelist.

"God's got a purpose for your life," he pointed out. My heart thumped. *A purpose? For me?* "God loves everybody," he continued. "There's nothing you've done or could do that would keep God from loving you. But you've got to receive him and believe in him. You know, one day we're all going to die. Every person in this room will die. I guarantee it. But if you'll give your life to Jesus, you'll live forever."

I thought about the times I either had tried to commit suicide or daydreamed about killing myself. My mind wandered back over all the drugs, drinking, crime, and shattered homes that had dominated my life. Maybe there was an answer—a way out of this mess. Maybe God was the answer. Maybe this evangelist wasn't such a goofball. After all, he had come from the streets of

Maybe there was an answer— a way out of this mess.

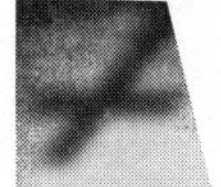

Houston, which was worlds bigger and tougher than Corpus Christi. If he could turn his life around, maybe I could too.

Rescued by the Cross

I began to weep as the evangelist neared the end of his message. All the emotional garbage of the past surfaced and melted my heart. I may have hardened myself on the outside, but inside I knew the truth: I was hurt. I wanted relief from the pain. Still, there was a fierce tug-of-war going on inside me. This evangelist's message had touched me, but I wasn't too sure of what was happening. When he asked everyone to bow their heads, I only half-bowed mine. I was determined to keep an eye on things.

"If you'd like to have what I have, stand up," he said.

Without thinking or realizing what I was doing, I stood. I could hear Jeff and some other guys around me sobbing and praying, "Save Ken Freeman, Lord. Help him." For the first time in my life, I didn't care what anyone else said. When Gage invited those who had stood up to walk to the altar where he was standing, I obeyed.

"Son, do you know you're a sinner?" he asked. The first thing I wanted to say was, "I'm not your son." Instead, I shook my head and sighed, "Sir, I don't know what I am. All I know is my mom wants me dead. She thinks I came from hell. I haven't seen my dad in more than a dozen years. I don't have a real family, and I've got a stepdad and a stepmom who drink. I've tried suicide. That's all I know. If this Jesus can make my life better, then I want to know him."

He guaranteed me Christ could do that.

"Will this Jesus ever leave me?" I asked.

"You might turn your back on him, but he will never turn his back on you."

That convinced me. At his urging, we knelt to pray. I would have done anything he asked, from turning cartwheels to performing jumping jacks. I trusted this guy. When he told me to confess my sins, it took a long time to tell God all the stuff I had done. "I'm asking you to forgive me," I concluded. "I don't understand all this, but I believe that you love me. I believe that you sent your Son to die on the cross for my sins. I believe in Jesus Christ as my Savior and Lord. I'm asking you to save me."

It took a long time to tell God all the stuff I had done.

When I finished praying, I felt as if a thousand pounds had been lifted off of me. My heart felt so

good, I wanted to jump through the ceiling. Suddenly I realized I was standing in the midst of the family I had always wanted. I was so happy I wanted to tell everybody about it. Although I hadn't been the baddest dude in school, I had been one of the most depressed, suicidal, self-pitying outcasts around. That's probably why I saw a stunned reaction on so many faces. Many were surprised enough to see me at church, but up front praying and claiming Christ as Savior? If God could reach me, he could reach anybody.

Despite their initial shock, people celebrated my decision, along with more than a dozen others who had gone to the altar. After the pastor introduced us, the audience broke out in tears and applause. Many gathered at the front of the church to hug us and share our joy. At first I hadn't cared for hugs, but now I didn't mind them one bit. I had never owned a Bible either, but after what Gage said about God's Word being the truth, I couldn't wait to read one. He said we needed to be baptized, and I did that too. I became a new man with a new life.

Brand-New Life

During the next few weeks, I began to understand more about what happened to me that night at church. I learned that the Holy Spirit caused me

to weep openly about my pain and to stand up when the evangelist called for decisions.

God wanted to forgive my sins so that I could spend eternity with him, but since I was a sinner, God couldn't let me into heaven. The only way I could be with God was to be perfect, like he is.

I learned that God made a special way for messed-up people like me to get into heaven. He sent his only Son, Jesus Christ, down to earth to live as a man. Jesus never messed up; he lived a perfect life. So when Jesus died on the cross two thousand years ago, God took all my sins and transferred them to Jesus. When Jesus died, he paid the full penalty for my sins. Then he rose from the dead to prove that all my sins were gone.

God provided a way for me to get into heaven. All I had to do was accept his gift of salvation by faith in Jesus Christ. When I knelt to pray with the evangelist, God saw my faith in Christ and—because of the Cross—he forgave all my sins.

Now I can say that I have truly been rescued by the Cross. God reached all the way down to a messed-up sixteen-year-old in the choir loft and gave me a brand-new life—one that still amazes, thrills, and satisfies me.

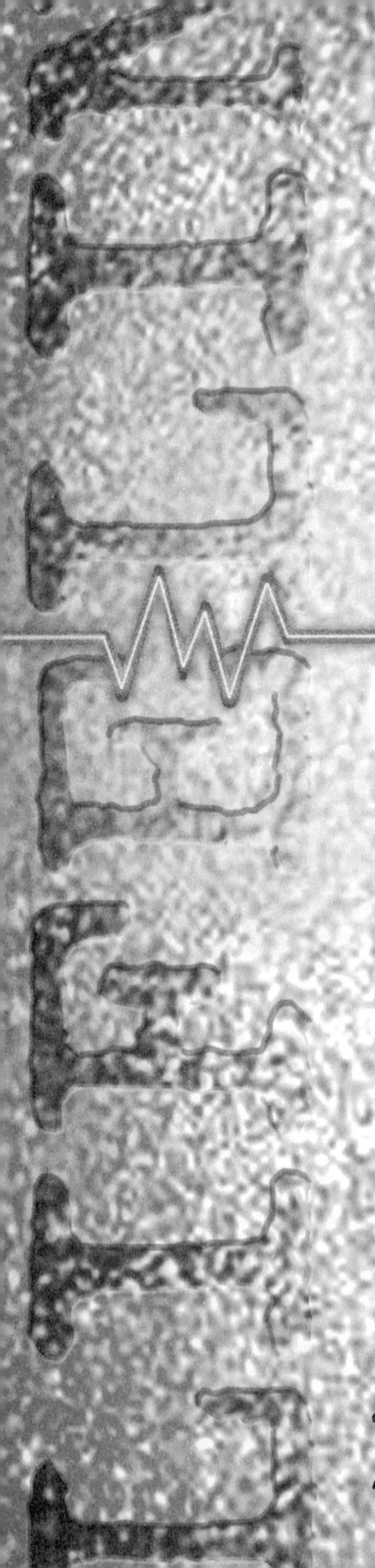

Take your everyday, ordinary life—your sleeping, eating, going-to-work, and walking-around life—and place it before God as an offering.

—Romans 12:1 *The Message*

LIFELINE

Living Proof

"Hey, that Christianity stuff is okay for you," you may be saying, "but why bother? I know church people. They're all a bunch of hypocrites. If you're trying to tell me that all I need is church to fix my problems, I don't believe you."

That's exactly how I used to feel. As I mentioned in the last chapter, before I gave my life to Jesus Christ, I was convinced that church members were just a bunch of slick con artists out to get money. It's amazing how we can reach such conclusions without ever setting foot inside a church or taking the time to become involved in one. The truth is that the less you know about something, the easier it is to form an opinion.

For those of you who are critical of churches, I have some startling news: Eternal life doesn't come from church membership. The only way you can have your sins forgiven and spend eternity in heaven is to accept Jesus Christ as your Savior and Lord. When you surrender your life to Jesus Christ, you can have a personal relationship with him. This relationship grows deeper and stronger the more you spend time with God in prayer, reading the Bible, and becoming involved in church. You see, going to church isn't a requirement for salvation; it is a way to grow in your relationship with Christ.

Besides, we should love the church because Jesus does. He wants us to be part of a local congregation so that we can find strength, support, encouragement, and helpful insights through our relationships with other believers. Sure, churches have faults. Nothing with humans in it will ever be perfect. I still remember the time I asked God to show me the location of a perfect church. He said, "If you want to join a perfect church, find one that has no people. But since you are not a perfect person, as soon as you join, it won't be perfect anymore."

God instituted the church. The church is not a building, even though these structures provide a place to meet and serve others. But if every one of

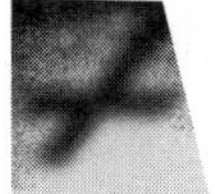

these buildings vanished tomorrow, the church would still exist. The true church is made up of people who believe in Jesus Christ as Savior and Lord. If you are a Christian, everywhere you go, the church goes with you.

Constantly criticizing the church comes from a spirit of pessimism. Fortunately, accepting Christ gave me a new outlook. Instead of being negative about everyone and every situation I encountered, my relationship with Christ helped me become optimistic. Instead of seeing people as bodies who were out to use me or get in my way, I began to see them as real people with real hurts, especially other kids who had gotten beaten up by life and were desperate for peace and guidance. Life deals hard knocks to everyone. How we deal with these setbacks makes all the difference.

Thirty years after accepting Christ as my Savior, I still have problems, but now I have a personal relationship with Someone who helps me overcome these problems. You see, in addition to forgiveness of sins and eternal life in heaven, there are many practical benefits to living for Jesus Christ. Instead of waking up with an aching head and a bad case of garbage mouth, I now sleep soundly and never wake up with a hangover. While it took awhile to shed my smoking habit, I have stopped smoking cigarettes and can now breathe clearly. I don't look over my shoulder anymore when I walk down the street, because I'm not afraid the police are looking for me. I don't have constant clashes and conflicts with people, because I stopped criticizing them and started communicating with them.

My life didn't change overnight. Becoming more like Jesus Christ takes a lot of time—and a lot of hard work. Although I received the gift of salvation the moment I knelt in that church in Corpus Christi and prayed for God to forgive my sins and come into my life, I still had a lot of bitterness and pain to deal with. The deep scars from my childhood were the result of sixteen years of abuse and neglect, so it took a long time for me to overcome these hurts. But I soon realized that in order to experience the joy and peace of my new life in Christ, I had to release my pent-up hatred and anger toward my parents.

In order to experience the joy and peace of my new life in Christ, I had to release my pent-up hatred and anger toward my parents.

Forgiveness

After I became a Christian, I started attending the youth group at the Second Baptist Church in Corpus Christi. I began to hang out with new friends, like Jeff McGowan and other Christian guys whose

character I admired. But when my stepfather had to move away from Corpus Christi unexpectedly, I was forced to move back to the Saint Louis area to live with my mother. I didn't want to leave my new church and Christian friends, but I didn't have a choice. I was very bitter toward my mother, who was too busy with alcohol and parties even to notice that I had come back. Without a church or any Christian friends in Saint Louis, I began to drift back into my former rebellious lifestyle.

When I turned seventeen, I got a strange phone call from a couple I had met at church in Corpus Christi. Though I didn't know them well, they invited me to live with them and offered me a free plane ticket. Mom obviously didn't care, and since I figured that living with this couple couldn't be any worse than living with my drunken mother, I went.

In the short time I stayed with them, Malcolm and Johnie Grainger were the kind of parents I had always wanted. I affectionately call them my "Jesus parents." They were the complete opposite of almost everyone I had ever known. After carefully watching their example for several months, I was truly amazed that people like the Graingers actually existed. They never swore or drank, and they prayed about everything. I used to joke that God lived in their bedroom. They would go up into that

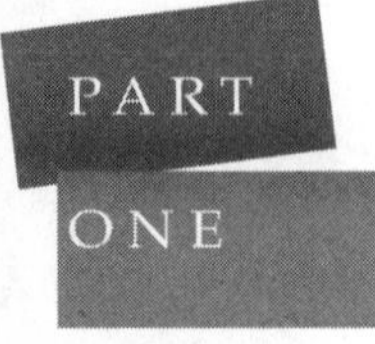

room and come out telling me something I needed to hear. "God told us . . ." they would begin as they outlined corrective steps for me. I will always be thankful for the way the Graingers helped me understand what having a personal relationship with God is all about: I could almost picture God sitting in their bedroom in a big red chair, ready to give me counsel.

One night as I was talking with the Graingers, I couldn't escape the gnawing feeling that, even though I was a Christian, something was still missing in my life. After we chatted awhile and Malcolm asked some probing questions, he confronted me with my main problem. "Ken," he asked, "do you love your parents?"

My eyes narrowed to slits, and I clenched my jaw. Looking straight into his eyes, I declared, "Love 'em? Are you kidding? How can I love my parents after everything they did to me? No way. I hate 'em."

"You know, Ken," Malcolm said, shaking his head, "there's a verse in the Bible that says you can't love God and hate your brother at the same time. You can't love Someone you have never seen and hate your brother whom you see all the time. You can't expect God to hear your prayers if you're holding on to hatred in your heart. You're going to

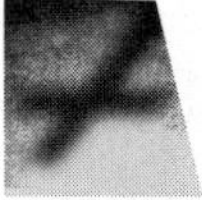

have to forgive your mother and father for all the things they have done. You don't have to agree with what they did, but you have to forgive them. You've got to get rid of all the bondage that's holding you back."

After we talked, I knelt on the floor beside the Graingers for one of the most emotionally gut-wrenching times in my life. My tears flowed as they prayed for me. I asked God to help me forgive my parents because I didn't know how. I asked him to forgive me for hating my mother, my father, and myself. All of my pent-up guilt, blame, and anger finally came to the surface. Malcolm and Johnie prayed some more, and I cried. Then I prayed, and they cried. This emotional release continued for more than two hours. When we were finished, I felt as if a load of garbage had been taken from my back. I was finally set free from my past. I no longer cared about getting an apology from my parents: I wanted to ask them to forgive me for hating them.

Though it was nearly midnight, I reached for the telephone and dialed my mother's number. When she answered in a slurred voice, I knew she

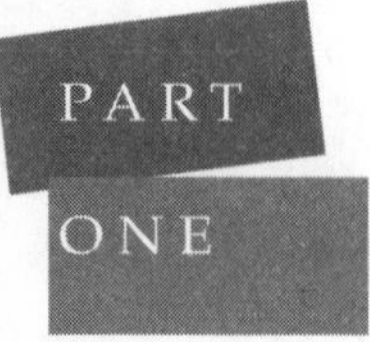

was drunk—as usual. I made sure she knew who I was before saying anything else.

"Mom, I know you're not going to understand this, but I am tired of hating you. Would you forgive me?"

She didn't say anything at first, but I soon realized she was weeping. "I'm so sorry things turned out the way they did," she finally mumbled, apologizing for not being the kind of mother she should have been.

"I love you, Mom," I said after an awkward silence. "Talk to you later."

Although I hadn't seen him in twelve years, I knew that my father was living in California. Since the West Coast was two hours behind Texas, I decided to see if I could get through. But when I dialed directory assistance, the operator said, "I'm sorry, sir, but that party has an unlisted number."

"Well, please listen," I urged and briefly explained the reason I wanted to talk to him. As I was talking, I burst into tears. The operator started crying, too, and said, "I could get in trouble if I put you through."

"Ma'am," I pleaded, "if you don't put me through to my dad, I think God's going to do something bad to you."

The next thing I heard was a telephone ringing.

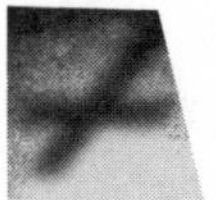

"Hello," a male voice answered.

"Hello," I said.

"Who's this?"

"This is Kenneth Wayne Freeman, your oldest son. Your first child."

"What do you want?" my father asked in a deadpan tone of voice.

"Well, I don't want your money," I said, thinking that might be the first thing that crossed his mind. "You don't even have to be my dad. But there are a few things I'd like to tell you."

I explained where I was living and related there had been some changes in my life. Then I described how I had hated him for years. Assuring him I didn't want to get into all the details, I explained that I wanted him to forgive me for hating him. He didn't ever have to see me, I said, my voice trembling, but I would like to see him at least once.

His response sent a chill up my spine.

Click.

Closure

While it hurt for my father to hang up on me, I wasn't angry because I had already forgiven him. Three weeks later, a manila envelope arrived in the Graingers' mailbox, filled with several photographs. A brief letter inside explained: "Ken, you're

not my son. I'm not your dad. It's never going to be that way. Here are some pictures. They're the last memories I have of you, but they're yours. I want you to stay out of my life." He signed it with his first name.

I cried a little. My father's letter brought a chapter of my life to a close. Through my tears I admired the pictures taken many years earlier. In one of them, my father held me in his arms. In another picture, our family stood together, smiling. I mourned the separation of our family and what the future wouldn't bring. It took awhile for the pain to subside, but I had to move on. The past was over.

Years later I met his wife, whom I think of as my stepmother though we've never had much of a relationship. Somehow my sister, Donna, located our father and visited him. She told him where I had settled since the night I asked for Dad's forgiveness. On a trip through the South, my stepmother stopped to see my wife, Debbie, and me. At our home, she laid out some of the missing pieces of the puzzle.

"Your father's a good man, Ken," she said. "He's been in the navy. I know you don't understand, but he got terribly frustrated when you and your sister came to visit after the divorce. You two were always whining and complaining about the things your

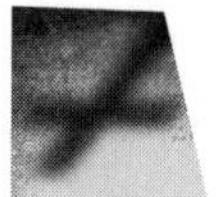

mother told you about him, and you asked him why he hated your mother. He just didn't know how to handle it. If he couldn't have you in his home, then he just wanted to act as if you had never been born. That may not have been the right thing to do, but that's the way it was. I'm sorry."

Miracle Meeting

After that conversation with my stepmother, I was convinced that my father would never speak to me again. Although I was disappointed that my father didn't want to have a relationship with me, I decided that I would continue to love him and pray for him. But in the summer of 1998, something wonderful happened.

After my older son, Josh, married, he decided to surprise me by tracking down my father for a reunion. When Josh finally located and contacted him, my father said he wasn't ready to meet me but would think about it. In the meantime, Dad corresponded with Josh and sent gifts to Josh's son—his great-grandson.

Two years after Josh's initial contact with my father, I called home to check my messages and was shocked to hear Dad's voice on the answering machine! He said that he was finally ready to talk to me and would like to meet me again. Overcome with emotion, I struggled to be strong and keep my voice calm over the phone with my father as we arranged a time and place to meet. After forty-two years, I was finally going to see my dad again! It was a miracle!

Anxiously awaiting this reunion, I boarded a plane with my wife, son, and daughter-in-law in July and headed to California. During the flight, I thought about how much I had missed my father and began to cry for all the lost years. When we arrived, however, I was determined to be strong for my family and for my dad.

When I first saw my father, I didn't know whether to hug him or merely shake his hand. I learned that he had been married to the same woman for forty-one years, and he told me that I had another half brother and half sister. While the meeting was somewhat awkward, we cried and prayed together, and I shared the Gospel with him.

After forty-two years, I was finally going to see my dad again!

Unfortunately, Dad had convinced himself that he was too old and too accustomed to his rebellious ways to change.

The opportunity to see and talk to my dad one more time has been one of the most healing experiences of my Christian life. I finally came face to face with the hurt and rejection of my past, and I was able to express to my father that I loved him and forgave him for rejecting us. I am still praying that one day he will embrace the life-changing message of the Cross so that I will see him again in heaven.

TRANSFORMED LIFE

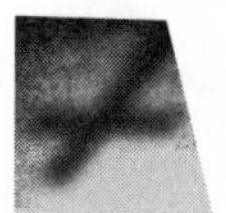

Now that I have finally forgiven both of my parents, I am free to get on with my life. I don't have to be chained to the past anymore, and neither do you. But here's the catch: You won't be able to forgive others until you have been forgiven by God. The kind of love it takes to forgive someone for deep wounds—like rejection, rape, physical abuse, neglect, divorce, and drug abuse—only comes from God. If you will let him have control of your life, he will give you the love you need to forgive others.

Why bother with all this Christianity stuff? Because it works. I'm living, breathing proof that faith in God is real. He took the mess of my life and transformed it into a message. Counseling didn't change me; God changed me. Although biblically based counseling does help people deal with personal issues and overcome the past, only Jesus Christ can change your life. If you're looking for hope, he's hope. If you're needing healing from

your emotional scars, he brings it. He will rescue you from your old life and give you a new one.

If you doubt that God is really able to change lives, contrast my life with my mother's: She was married ten times, which required countless adjustments and caused continuous upheaval in our home. I've been married once, for more than twenty-five years, and have stability and a love relationship that grows deeper with time. She had four children by two different men, and her family is now scattered across the country. Both of my sons came from the same marriage and live close to me—both are Christians and involved in church. My mother never really knew her grandchildren because she stayed in a drunken haze most of the time. My wife and I spend as much time as we can with our grandson, Canaan, who is one of the crowning joys of our life.

There are so many benefits to Christianity: peace instead of confusion; sobriety and calm instead of drunkenness and fights; a life of purpose and value instead of hopelessness and despair; a happy marriage instead of the pain of divorce; a future with a promise instead of doubt and fear over what is to come; friends instead of enemies; joy instead of anger; forgiveness instead of hatred, revenge, and bitterness; eternal life in heaven instead of eternal suffering in hell.

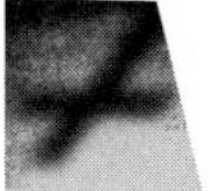

In spite of the difficulties I faced in childhood, I wouldn't change a thing about my experience. God has used my background for his good purpose (see Romans 8:28). Today I travel across the country with my message of hope and am able to reach many young people in public schools because of what I've been through. Everywhere I go, the reactions are similar: People relate to the pain in my background and find reassurance that someone identifies with their suffering. They know I understand the junk they are facing because I have lived through it.

Do you feel so defeated, hopeless, and full of despair that you're ready to throw in the towel? That is the best place to be if you want God to lift you out of the mire. When you are ready to throw up your hands and say, "I give up," then the Lord can take over. This kind of surrender is illustrated by a friend who bought his son a bag of chocolate-chip cookies from a vending machine. The young boy struggled to open the bag as they drove down the highway.

"Son, let Daddy help you with that," he urged.

"No! I can do it myself! No!"

The boy flailed away, turning, twisting, gritting his teeth, and failing to tear apart the hermetically sealed plastic. Twice more his father offered to help. Each time the boy shouted, "No! No, Daddy!"

Twenty minutes later, defeated and hungry, the boy finally asked, "Daddy, would you open the cookies for me?"

His father obliged. But every cookie in the bag had been reduced to crumbs. Had the boy simply given in and asked for help sooner, he could have had chocolate-chip cookies instead of crumbs. Likewise, if you refuse help from your heavenly Father and demand the right to run your life, it will disintegrate into little pieces. When you're at your wit's end, there is no way to look but up. When you choose to turn to God, you will avoid any more painful consequences of your stubbornness.

When I look back at my early life and consider where I was headed, I know I ought to be dead or in prison. But I was rescued by the Cross of Jesus Christ. My transformed life is powerful evidence of God's grace. I will never get over how his grace has changed my life. God's grace can change yours, too, if you will only let him. The good news is that God loves you as much as he loves me. If you'll allow him to rescue you, you will be amazed how he will lead you out of your past and into his purpose.

PART TWO

Stepping Out of Your Past

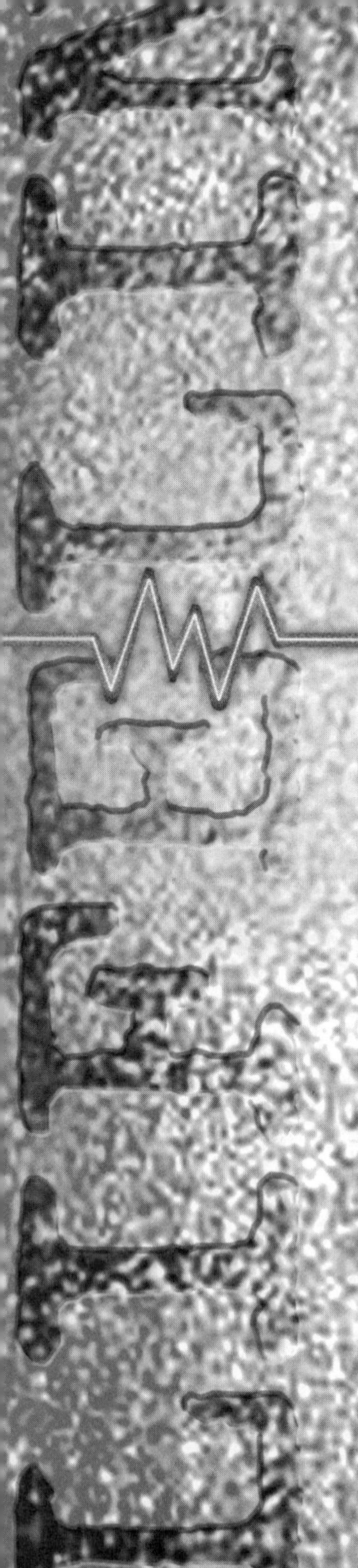

[Kill] off everything connected with [the] way of death: sexual promiscuity, impurity, lust, doing whatever you feel like whenever you feel like it, and grabbing whatever attracts your fancy. That's a life shaped by things and feelings instead of by God.

—Colossians 3:5 *THE MESSAGE*

LIFELINE

LSD (Lies, Sex, & Death)

Though only fourteen years old, the teenage lovers burned with passion. Other students watched them French kissing between classes. After school, they were inseparable and often entwined in a cuddling embrace. All were likely signs of sexual intimacy. Concerned about their daughter's overly intense relationship with this young man, her parents asked her to stop seeing him: "You can be his friend, but we don't want you to date him."

What happened next shocked the community and made newspaper headlines: "Forbidden to date, sweethearts leaped into a canal." The couple drowned themselves because they thought they couldn't live without seeing each other. But at their

age they hadn't experienced enough of life to understand the depth of love required for a lifelong commitment. True love doesn't find fulfillment at the bottom of a canal, the sharp point of a knife, or the wrong end of a gun.

One of their teachers gave me the suicide notes these Florida teens left behind. Ripe with emotion, they tell a sad tale. The young man wrote to his friends:

> I'm taking my life because without [her], I have no life. I cannot go on living. . . . There's something that hurts me very deep inside. I'll remember all of you. None of you will be forgotten. Please don't forget me. I put in my best these fourteen years I've been on this hell-hole of earth. . . . I'm not leaving you. I'm leaping from the realm of reality into the darkness unknown. Funny, [a friend] was talking about suicide earlier. I never thought it would have anything to do with me. So say farewell to all. As the immortal Beethoven once said, "Applaud, friend. The comedy is over."

His girlfriend wrote to her parents:

> Mom and Dad, you'll never understand the

> love between [us]. Why is it you were never able to understand me or that you lived to make my life miserable? . . . You won't let me see him in this world. We're going to another place. I love you all very much. I'd like to ask you for forgiveness, but I know you'll never understand. This is all I want to tell you. I love him and I will always love him, but I will never be able to stay on this earth without him. Please don't cry for me. This is what I want. I want you to feel happy because I'm going to a place where I'll be with [him]. Lastly, I'm sorry I couldn't be with you all. I love you very much. . . . P.S. Thank you for everything you have given me in this life and thank you for loving me all my life, you all.

Suicide is a permanent solution to a temporary problem.

After signing this message, she jotted notes to about a dozen friends, dating each with the exact hour and minute. Just before two o'clock in the morning, she and her boyfriend jumped into deep water, thinking they were taking the easy way out. But, as the saying goes, suicide is a permanent solution to a temporary problem. Several years later, their parents, families, and friends

are still trying to pick up the pieces from this tragic loss.

Sadly, this young couple believed several lies. They believed the lie that they would be better off dead than separated. They actually thought they couldn't face life without each other and that they would never want to date another person for the rest of their lives. They foolishly thought the act of suicide would send them to a better place, but the Bible says they will face judgment instead (see Hebrews 9:27). The girl thought her parents lived solely to make her life miserable. Actually, they were deeply concerned about her getting too emotionally attached to this boy at too young an age. If they didn't care about her, they wouldn't have said a word.

Believing lies can have deadly consequences. This same sort of tragedy occurred with a young man I met in Arkansas. Though I didn't know him well, I had become friends with other members of his family. A senior in high school, he carried a straight-A average and seemed destined for greatness. He had only one stain on his background—a year earlier he had gotten his girlfriend pregnant. She kept the baby, and they planned to marry after he graduated from high school. Instead, one night he went home, put a gun to his head, and pulled the

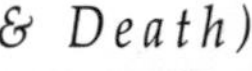

trigger. He left behind a note that essentially said, "I've made some bad choices. Maybe this will be better for everybody. It will be a lot easier."

This young man also believed lies. Nobody in his family had attacked or degraded him for his mistake. Yet his suicide had a dramatic impact that shattered more lives. Three weeks later his stepfather killed himself, leaving no suicide note or other clues. He had never given any indication of being depressed or upset enough to take his own life.

Those who believe suicide is a sensible option should meet the survivors of this double tragedy: the devastated teenage mother who sought counseling to cope with her anguish; the child who doesn't understand why Daddy left him; the mother and wife who crumbled emotionally and only survived because of her faith in God and the caring support of her family; and the young man's cousin, who cried almost every day for months.

Relationship Wrecks

Thanks to the lie that having a boyfriend or girlfriend is the measure of acceptability, many teens feel absolutely worthless when their relationships sour. That myth helps explain the sickening deaths of four young women in Oklahoma during the

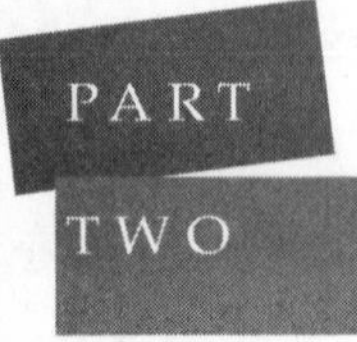

1997–98 school year. All four girls shot themselves to death because someone they were dating broke up with them. Each of them bought the lie: "Something must be wrong with me. I can't make it without this guy."

These four girls thought they were in love. But *love* is a heavy-duty word that involves self-sacrifice and long-term commitment, regardless of circumstances. After twenty-five years of marriage, I think I know something about love. But do teens really understand it? I don't deny that young people can care deeply about someone else and experience powerful feelings for that person. But true love includes serious responsibilities that are beyond the scope of teenagers, even those just shy of legal adulthood. Yet many teens toss this word around as casually as "Hello," "Good-bye," or "Call me some time."

I'm not implying that everyone who breaks up with their dating partner will commit suicide. But such shocking actions spring from deep-rooted emotions that often include sexual involvement.

Premarital sex has long-lasting implications. Counseling thousands of sexually active young people during my ministry, I have seen how sex outside of marriage deeply wounds and incapacitates young lives through loss of self-respect, disillusionment, emotional devastation, and deep-seated guilt. Plagued by insecurity and convinced that everyone is out to use them, many sexually active teens no longer trust anybody. They don't feel loved for their inner beauty or value—just what they can give physically.

Sometimes the sex is involuntary, which is even more damaging. One girl in Oklahoma had been raped, molested, and mistreated so many times she looked like a shell of a person. Even after becoming a Christian, she feared men. The night she heard my story, she burst into tears. Her pain led her to come talk with me. I'll never forget putting my arms around her in a fatherly hug and telling her, "I'm hugging you because I love you for who you are. This will be one of the first things you've gotten from a man who doesn't want anything from you." She sobbed and clung tightly to me. Every other man who ever hugged her wanted more.

Though this young woman had been forcibly violated, millions willingly give away their sexuality. This contradicts one of love's most significant elements: its exclusive nature. God's ideal is a faithful, lifelong partnership until parted by death.

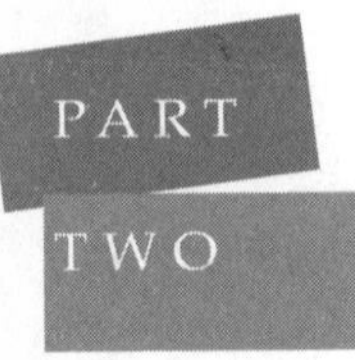

No matter how popular it is to lose your virginity, throwing away the precious gift of your body is wrong. The apostle Paul tells us to "put to death the sinful, earthly things lurking in you. Have nothing to do with sexual sin, impurity, lust, and shameful desires" (Colossians 3:5 NLT). "Sexual sin" is having sex without the benefit of marriage. In other words, living together before marriage is wrong. So is having premarital sex with your dates, extramarital affairs, and homosexual encounters. The same goes for sexual fondling and touching that includes everything but intercourse.

God's prohibition against adultery doesn't end with the Ten Commandments. Teachings against sexual immorality appear throughout the Bible:

> *You are to abstain from . . . sexual immorality.* You will do well to avoid [this]. (Acts 15:29, emphasis added)

> Let us behave decently, as in the daytime, not in orgies and drunkenness, *not in sexual immorality* and debauchery, not in dissension and jealousy. (Romans 13:13, emphasis added)

> The body is not meant for sexual immorality, but for the Lord, and the Lord for the

> body. . . . *Flee from sexual immorality.* All other sins a man commits are outside his body, but he who sins sexually sins against his own body. (1 Corinthians 6:13, 18, emphasis added)

> It is God's will that you should be sanctified: *that you should avoid sexual immorality;* that each of you should learn to control his own body in a way that is holy and honorable, not in passionate lust like the heathen, who do not know God. (1 Thessalonians 4:3–5, emphasis added)

> Marriage should be honored by all, and the marriage bed kept pure, for *God will judge the adulterer and all the sexually immoral.* (Hebrews 13:4, emphasis added)

Although the world often scoffs at good role models, one of the best is A. C. Green of the Dallas Mavericks. In 1997, Green broke a record by playing 907 consecutive games in the National Basketball Association. However, his most noteworthy record has spanned more than twelve thousand days—that is how long he has abstained from premarital sex. For a man in his mid-thirties to proclaim his virginity in public is admirable. But to

do so in professional sports, where sexual immorality is so common, takes real guts. I'm sure Green gets harassed, but guess what? He can sleep at night without worrying about whether his latest fling left him with an emotional hangover or a sexually transmitted disease, such as AIDS.

"Safe sex" is a myth invented by those who don't want to curb their sexual appetites. There is no such thing as safe sex. One study of married couples in which one partner was infected with AIDS found that 17 percent of the partners using condoms for protection still caught the disease within eighteen months.[1] That's one in six! Do you want to take that kind of risk? Some people mistakenly believe that the only way to get AIDS is through homosexual behavior, sharing dirty drug needles, or through a tainted blood transfusion. While those are the leading causes, they aren't the only ones. Sleeping around today is literally like playing Russian roulette.

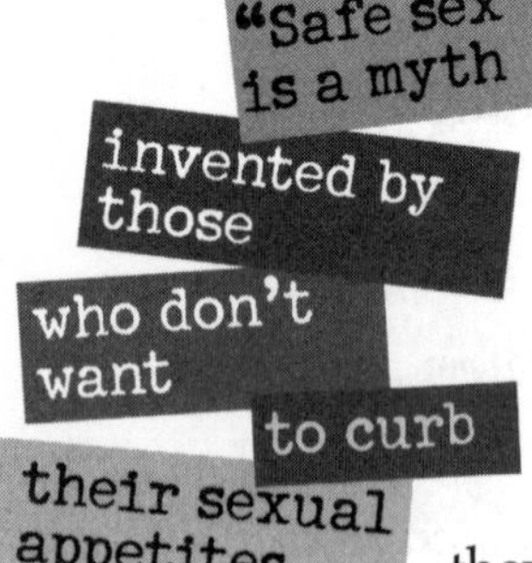

Still, countless numbers of young women have confessed to me they are having sex with their boyfriends—not because they want to, but because they hope to earn acceptance or fear these boyfriends will leave them. Well, girls, if a guy won't stick around unless you give in to his immoral desires, get rid of him! He doesn't really love you, no matter what he says.

"Just Once Won't Hurt"

I have counseled many young women who still struggle with overwhelming guilt from having abortions. These women believed the lie that "having sex just once won't hurt." That one sexual encounter led to pregnancy, and their choice to "resolve" their problem by having an abortion simply made matters worse. The scars of that incident will stay with them for years. Premarital sex and abortion both go against God's Word. The damage to countless people affected by these unbiblical practices is immeasurable.

It's bad enough that so many encourage sex outside of marriage, but society compounds the problem by reinforcing one mistake with another. Today young women can obtain birth control pills and abortions without their parents' knowledge (yet authorities need parental permission to dispense an aspirin). Some schools also pass out condoms, encouraging promiscuity under the guise of protecting students. Believing lies for the past thirty years has thoroughly eroded our nation's moral standards.

Lies affect our lives in countless other ways.

When my mother was fifteen years old, she believed her friends when they encouraged her to take a drink. They promised "just one" wouldn't hurt—that was a lie. Sure, maybe one drink wouldn't have hurt too much, if she drank one beer and never touched alcohol again as long as she lived. But her first drink as a teenager plunged her into the alcoholism that ruined her life and led straight to her grave.

There is a strong possibility that "just one drink" will have the same effect on you. Maybe you won't go off the deep end like my mother, but you can still find yourself in deep trouble when one drink leads to two. The next time may be five, six, eight, or ten. It could take several years for you to progress to all-night booze parties, but if you're headed in the wrong direction—no matter how fast you are going—you can still plunge over that cliff. Drinking is especially hazardous for young teens. According to the National Institute on Alcohol Abuse and Alcoholism, people who start drinking before age fifteen are four times as likely to develop alcohol dependence or alcoholism than those who begin at twenty-one. In addition, the kind of alcohol abuse that leads to impaired lives is more than twice as likely to occur for those who start drinking at earlier ages.[2]

This 1998 report reflects sobering truths about alcohol. Yet millions still believe the lie that liquor is nothing more than a pleasant way to relax. Many of them will pay the terrible consequences. Two of my stepfathers went to early graves because they believed that lie. My sister, Donna, is penniless, going nowhere, and trapped in an empty, unfulfilling life because she, too, swallowed that lie.

For many years I also believed lies—especially ones my mother told: I came from hell, nobody wanted me, and I would never amount to anything. Believing those statements led me to attempt suicide, drink, smoke, steal, cheat, and tell my own lies. After all, if I was worthless, what difference did anything make? I was convinced that nothing mattered, so that is the way I lived.

Millions of young people and adults are stuck in similar patterns. They've bought into lies about themselves. These lies lead to sin, and sin leads to death—not just physical death, but also emotional death. The end of relationships or a shattered career can turn your time on earth into a living catastrophe. That is why you must read God's Word and discover the truth that will strengthen your immunity to lies.

Knowing the truth will help you avoid myths. Just because you grew up in a broken home or a

dysfunctional environment—just because your father ignored you, your mother abused you, a relative raped you, or you got pregnant in high school—doesn't mean you have to remain imprisoned by these wounds. The idea that you have no chance of leaving your past behind is nothing but a lie from Satan. Jesus called the devil "a liar and the father of lies" (John 8:44). Satan has lied from the beginning of time and doesn't know how to tell the truth.

Fortunately, truth will prevail. No matter how many people try to twist, distort, or suppress it, truth will emerge victorious. Not too long ago, I led a crusade at a university in Texas. At one meeting attended mostly by Christians, I felt led to skip the message I had planned to deliver and have a heart-to-heart talk with the group. After I exhorted students to reinforce their commitment to Christ and maintain high standards, a young woman walked to the podium. "I need to talk to the group," she said. I nodded for her to continue.

"When I was sixteen I started dating a guy, and last year, when I was a senior in high school, we got engaged," she said, her voice trembling slightly. "We had never had sex, never even touched each other, though

we had dated for a couple of years. We got engaged, and about three weeks later we slept together. He convinced me that he loved me. He said we were going to get married anyway, so what difference did it make? Well, guess what happened? After we had sex a couple of times, he said he didn't want to marry me anymore. But I want my purity back. I want to make a commitment now that I will never have sex again until I'm married."

Students gathered around and prayed for her. When I returned to campus the next day for a prayer meeting, someone had left a note of encouragement for the young woman on the bulletin board. The anonymous writer had pinned a white carnation to the note as a symbol of the purity God had returned to her. This woman made a mistake, but she didn't let that mistake keep her locked in chains.

No Regrets

I've met other students who struggle to overcome immoral pasts. A young mother from Louisiana spent a week as a counselor at one of my summer camps. She wept bitterly during one of my services and afterward came with a friend to see me. They had partied together in college, sometimes driving four or five hours to live it up. For

each of them, having premarital sex had been as casual as drinking a beer.

"You know, if I could only have come to my senses sooner . . . ," she said. "If I could have just listened to somebody sooner . . ."

Although she had gotten married, her past mistakes had cost her dearly, tainting her reputation, values, and self-image. She had hated going home during college breaks because she knew she was lying to her unsuspecting parents. Both she and her friend now live with regret, a paralyzing feeling that can take years to overcome.

Sometimes people stray because that is what they are taught, like a young man I met in Florida. He had slept with dozens of women before becoming a Christian. When I asked why, he replied, "My dad encouraged me. He said that real men drink and go to bed with women. And the more women you go to bed with, the more you become a man." His idea of becoming a real man was bedding girls, not wedding a special partner whom he loved.

What a sad legacy his father had created. I meet kids all the time whose parents are sleeping around. The kids' parents drop them off at church for some good moral instruction and when the kids come home, their mother's in bed with some stranger.

Take the woman from Texas whose son is repeat-

ing her teenage mistake three decades later. Charmed by a high-school football hero, she ended up having sex with him before they were married. Steady alcohol consumption gradually turned her "hero" into an abusive alcoholic who eventually committed suicide. Instead of learning from her past, this woman got involved in a sexual relationship with another alcoholic, eventually married him, and drifted away from church.

Her son knew that his mother had been sleeping with his stepfather before their marriage, so he saw nothing wrong with shacking up with his girlfriend. When this mother asked me, "What am I going to do about him?" I couldn't help thinking, *You set the standard for him when he saw what kind of life you were living.* This story came to a tragic end with the young man's death in an alcohol-related car crash.

As long as you are alive, it is never too late to change your behavior.

However, as long as you are alive, it is never too late to change your behavior. Remember the college student who had been sexually active but decided to change her ways after becoming a Christian? Today she is married to a pastor. God has blessed her in many ways. While she wishes she hadn't been sexually active, she finally made peace with herself. During her engagement to her husband, they remained pure. Their

sexual intimacy came at the right time—after the wedding vows.

Our younger son, Jeremy, is a virgin. Fortunately, this is no longer an oddity, thanks to the impact of the True Love Waits movement. What began as the object of scorn and ridicule in the early nineties has spread across the world and become an accepted part of mainstream society. This movement offers mutual encouragement to young people who want to abstain from premarital sex.

I don't know if Jeremy would have the strength to refrain from sexual immorality without the positive reinforcement from his three college roommates. They hold each other accountable not to put themselves in compromising situations. I've been around them when they're with their girlfriends. It is a treat to watch young men and women treat each other with respect and dignity. Each of them will have a special gift to share with their children one day. They will honestly be able to say, "You are special enough to wait for your wife as I waited for your mother."

Lust always makes you feel guilty and cheap. Love makes you feel good and peaceful.

Their actions demonstrate the difference between lust and love. Lust always makes you feel guilty and cheap. Love makes you feel good and peaceful. Love is more than going to movies and eating from the same bucket of popcorn or getting gooey-eyed over the good-looking object of your affections. Love involves purity, giving, making the right choices, and accepting responsibility. It includes maintaining high standards, open communication, tenderness, and caring. Best of all, it's the kind of gift you can give—and receive—with no regrets.

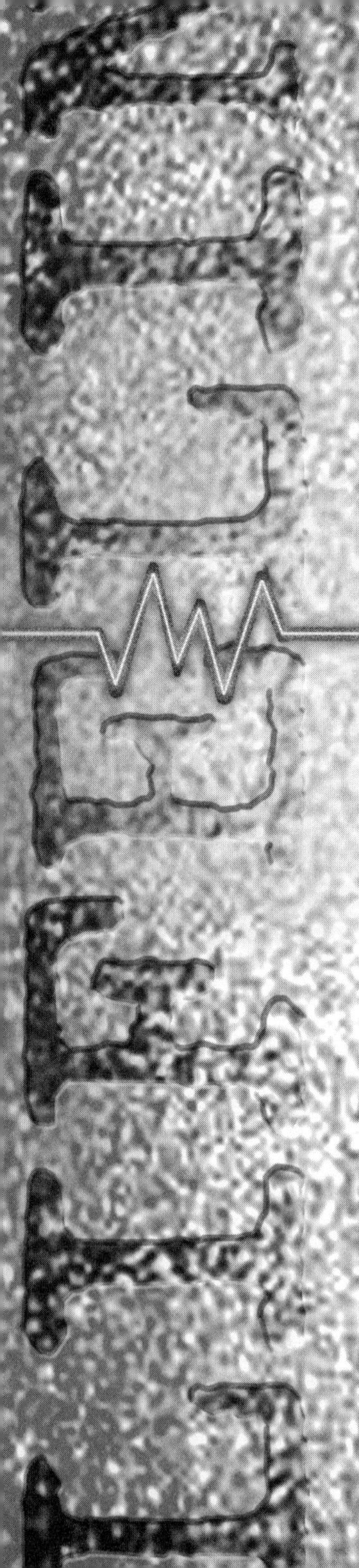

God hates . . . a troublemaker in the family.

—Proverbs 6:16, 19 *The Message*

LIFELINE

6 Home Wreckers

Though divorce is often portrayed as the ultimate solution to damaged relationships, it only marks the beginning of trouble for its innocent victims. No matter what the outcome for Mom or Dad, or how relieved they might be, the children always lose. They are too young to grasp the concept of their home splitting apart. Most struggle to cope with the pain. While some children may recognize what happened, accepting it is a different story.

I've met thousands of young people from broken homes who remain haunted by this ugly reality years later. Their parents tried to justify their failure to honor their wedding vows with such excuses as: "We were just never meant to be together," "I just couldn't

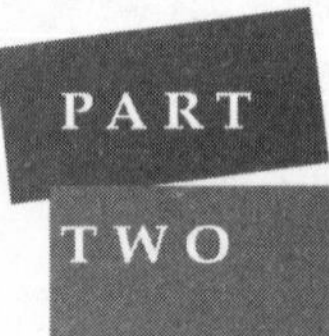

handle the pressure anymore," "I wasn't happy. Don't I deserve the right to be happy?" and "We just grew apart. Nothing is meant to last forever."

These decisions commonly leave innocent children with lifelong scars, especially when the parent who gains custody walks out on other commitments. That was the case with a beautiful young woman I met in Louisiana. She had never known her father. Eight months earlier, her mother left for work one morning and never returned home.

Despite her physical attractiveness, Tiffany didn't feel pretty—just angry, confused, and dismayed. She couldn't understand why her father never came to see her or why her mother deserted her. She felt totally alone, a state I could readily identify with. Tiffany was also at risk: Without some kind of relief from this pressure, she was likely to search for refuge in drugs and alcohol. Although she had never partied, she admitted that lately she had given it some thought.

"How do you make it without your parents?" she asked me, tears streaming down her face. "How do you do that?"

Equally sad is the story of the high-school senior I met a few years ago in Arkansas. Though a popular cheerleader, Joanne grappled with the continuing aftermath of her parents' divorce. Both

abandoned her when she was a child. An aunt and uncle took her in, but her uncle molested her several times. When the crime came to light, a social service agency relocated her to another home. Though finally living in healthy circumstances, she battled fear, anxiety, anger, and jealousy of others who came from healthy homes.

"You know, I'm never going to be a daddy's little girl," Joanne sighed. "I don't know what it's like to have a mom and dad. I've kind of been kicked around." She often told fellow students, "Don't take having a mom and dad for granted. Because until you're without them, you don't know what it feels like."

Some believe divorce signals physical or sexual abuse in the home. That isn't necessarily true. While Joanne had been abused, Tiffany had not. Yet a lack of physical abuse doesn't diminish the impact of the emotional damage. Both of them had been neglected, one of the worst forms of mistreatment. Their parents didn't raise and train the children they had brought into this world. Their failure left these young women struggling to understand the meaning of love and family.

One young man I met two years ago lamented how his life wasn't fair. His dark eyes appeared empty, as if he were merely a shell of a person. Both parents had left him behind years ago after their divorce. While another family took him in, he was barely hanging on. Never knowing the love of a mother or father had left him bitter and hostile. Since his parents didn't care about him, he told me, he didn't care about them. "I don't know who they are or where they are," he said. Pausing as his eyes clouded over, he asked the question that lingers in so many minds of today's younger generation: "Why don't parents care? Why is it that adults are so screwed up and screw our lives up?"

I know what it's like to feel as if you're living with strangers who don't care about you. My mother would be gone for days or even weeks, occasionally stopping long enough to grab a change of clothes or popping in with another person. We never knew who would be coming through the front door—a stepfather, former stepfather, ex-boyfriend, or a new fling.

I know what it's like to feel as if you're living with strangers who don't care about you.

Slowly Sinking

Judging by my visits to hundreds of public schools every year, the problem of divorce is getting worse. In the past, when I asked how many students came from broken homes, about half the kids raised their hands. Lately it's closer to two-

thirds. At one student assembly, I asked, "How many of you don't know your dads?" About a third from the divorced group kept their hands up. That is close to one-fourth of the student body coming from homes with no visible father figure.

Having experienced this void, I know what a gaping hole it leaves in each of those young lives. And society wonders why we struggle with juvenile drug abuse, crime, and delinquency! Without a rudder, a ship will wander aimlessly and crash into shore. A society without stable homes and strong fathers is like a rudderless ship, slowly sinking into a morass of immorality and personal problems. Without correction, our nation will be overwhelmed.

The good news is we still have time to reverse our aimless drift. There is hope for the future. A prime example is Jordan, an eighth-grade student I met when I spoke at his school in Oklahoma. I wasn't surprised when he came up after the assembly, eyes blazing. My story usually stirs predictable reactions: The girls start sobbing and the guys get angry. Jordan tapped a finger in my chest that felt like a hot poker. "Man, how do you know?" he spat, his earrings bobbing off his shoulder-length hair and denim jacket. "How do you know how I feel? How do you know what I'm going through?"

Given his reputation as the school troublemaker, teachers were surprised he was even talking to me. He eventually got around to bragging about his drug and alcohol use and how he had whipped other guys with sets of chains. He also talked about fighting with his father, who liked to whip him with a belt buckle. After his parents divorced, Jordan got in fistfights with some of his mother's boyfriends after they punched her.

"Listen, dude, I've had nine stepfathers," I told him, sending shock waves through his eyes. "I've been through a lot of the same stuff. Why don't you come listen to me tonight? I'll tell you a lot more about my background."

"Well, I don't have a ride," he replied, but a church member standing nearby said, "I'll come by and pick you up."

"Okay," Jordan nodded. "I'm comin'."

Jordan's reaction to the Gospel was the same as mine—on his first visit to church, he broke down, cried like a baby, and accepted Christ as his Savior. Whoever doesn't believe God is real has never seen a person's countenance change like a rainbow popping out after a cloudburst. Jordan's sullen, grouchy, despair-ridden face brightened with hope and optimism. In the twinkling of an eye, everything seemed different. He knew he could make it.

Determination and hope are necessary ingredients for a person to declare, "I can fight back. I can make it. I can win." Bleak situations don't spell inevitable doom. Various studies have shown that cancer patients who glumly accept death as their only option are likely to see a self-fulfilling prophecy, while those with an optimistic outlook have an increased chance of recovery. Divorce is our society's emotional cancer, creating hate, rage, confusion, anger, and blame that turns into a monster. Those from divorced homes are at greater risk of going through divorce as adults. But with the right approach, you can overcome these odds.

Tearing Down Strongholds

In his book *The Three Battlegrounds,* Francis Frangipane defines a stronghold as "a house made of thoughts," encouraging us to tear these houses down. Just like lust, drugs, or anorexia, divorce is a stronghold we must attack. The church is presently losing the battle: Statistics show that evangelical Christians' marriages are breaking up at a faster rate than those of nonbelievers.

But we can defeat the enemy of divorce, using spiritual ammunition. The Bible says that Christians are given spiritual weapons that have "the divine power to demolish strongholds" (2 Corinthians

10:4). Jesus can defeat the strongholds in your life, but first you have to let him come into your life.

Everything we do affects how we think, feel, and act. Some young people love the beat of rap, metal, or rock music. But if the lyrics to that music glorify premarital sex, drugs, and rebellion, they set up spiritual strongholds in the listener. The same goes for violent, bloody, sadistic video games or movies that many see as harmless fantasies, or dance clubs where drinking and sexual connections are the prime order of the evening. While I'm not against having fun, if your fun is leading you down the wrong path, you need to walk a different way.

It reminds me of the fifth-grade teacher who delivered a profound message after one of my assemblies. I usually speak to older students, but I'm glad I had the opportunity to hear her wise warning: "If you're in the fifth grade and you're making Cs and Ds, that's the kind of life you're going to have," she said. "When you graduate from high school or college, you'll have a C or D life. Right now, you're determining that about your future."

She was right on track. If you're content with your situation and aren't willing to make an effort to change, then that's the way you will live. Don't complain about being stuck in an unhappy mar-

riage, lousy job, or below-average relationships if you're not willing to do anything to improve. Life is tough. Millions of people are looking for easy steps to success, but the truth is, they don't exist.

Too many Christians run around saying, "You just have to trust in God." While that is true, it is only the beginning. We can't just sit around and wait for blessings to fall into our lap. God doesn't wave a magic wand and remove all our problems. He gives us the tools, but we have to use them.

This reminds me of the pastor who visited a juvenile detention center for the first time. Before going in to see the kids, he met with an officer who confided that he had several personal problems. He figured the preacher might have some worthwhile insights to share. Smiling, the pastor said, "Well, all I can tell you is that you just need to trust God. Just trust him."

That glib answer didn't satisfy the juvenile officer, who was looking for helpful advice on a few practical steps he could take. "No, really," he frowned.

"That's it," the preacher said, dismissing the officer's problems with a wave of his hand. "If you'll just trust God, you'll be okay. Just trust him."

After they talked awhile, the officer saw he wasn't making any progress, so he escorted the

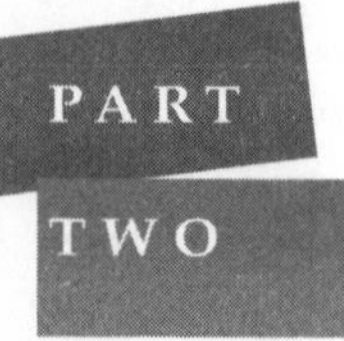

pastor to the holding cell. Twenty juvenile delinquents milled around, grumbling and swearing at each other. As they walked inside, the guard said, "The door doesn't have a knob on it. When you're finished, you just have to knock on the door, and we'll let you out."

The door clanged shut. The pastor nervously looked around. This collection of characters, whose scarred bodies were decorated with tattoos and earrings, was a little tougher than he had imagined. When he talked about Christ, they responded with hoots, catcalls, and laughter. A few even threatened to hurt him. After fifteen agonizing minutes, beads of sweat ran down the pastor's forehead. He knew he couldn't get out on his own.

Suddenly he spotted a telephone and dialed the front desk. When the officer answered, he asked, "What can I do to help these kids?"

"Well, pastor," the man drawled, "you've just got to trust God, you know. Just trust him."

Yes, we must trust God. But we also must move forward with him. You must choose to climb out of the slop and walk with God. Some people like living in misery. They enjoy pain, conflict, screaming, and fighting. It makes their lives exciting and provides them with a ready-made excuse for why they can never do any better. They also love to encour-

age others to wallow in the same muck. Just call a pity party and watch who brings the cups, punch, and cookies.

If you come from a dysfunctional background and have never dealt with the consequences of your past, you may need to seek professional counseling from a pastor or Christian therapist. Even confiding in a close friend can sometimes help you through your pain. Forget the myth that you can heal yourself. If anger burns beneath your tough exterior, you'd better get rid of it before you are consumed by the fire. Life isn't football practice where you just "suck it up" and get better.

Honesty was one of the most effective weapons in combating my past. As I mentioned before, I used to endure mood swings that hurled me through feelings of happiness, anger, jealousy, sadness, and isolation—all in the space of fifteen minutes. To get over things like this, I had to talk openly with others. It helps to find people who can encourage you—especially others who have been there, done that, and worn the T-shirt.

Forget the myth that you can heal yourself.

Breaking the Chain

Despite my mother's multiple marriages and my lack of good role models as a boy, I have broken the

chain of divorce that plagued my family—with lots of help. Living with the Graingers brought me face to face with positive, godly people. I also saw healthy families at church and among my new friends. Suddenly I met teens whose parents had always been around, unlike the street kids I had hung with in the past. I saw clear choices set before me: Win or lose? Love or hate? Heal or hurt? Good or bad? Life or death?

Learning to make the right decisions took years. For example, my marriage got off to a bumpy start because of miscommunication. I finally sought out a pastor who taught me some valuable communication skills that helped me deal with the effects of my childhood. He taught me that the three major causes of divorce are problems with communication, sex, and money. If just one of those areas is out of balance, he said, it will affect the other two. Failing to resolve these issues leaves you a prime candidate for a split.

If life deals you setbacks, you still get to choose how to deal with them. There is nothing sadder than someone who gets a second chance and walks away from it. I've seen kids go through horrible situations before being placed in a new home or adopted by a caring stepparent. Then, when they enjoy a stable environment, they go wild. They break into houses,

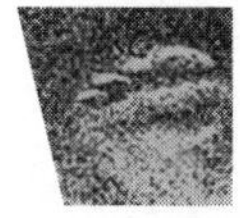

abuse drugs, get others pregnant (or get pregnant themselves), and throw away their future.

Everyone makes their own choices. Given that truth, you can't go through life blaming your parents for all your problems, even if they are divorced. Doing so is a sure method for ignoring your responsibilities and repeating your parents' mistakes. Instead, when you reach an age of accountability, you must decide whether to cling to the past or learn from it. If you come from a broken home, vow never to subject your children to the uncertainty, insecurity, and fear that wracked your childhood.

Dealing with the grief of divorce is important if you hope to avoid carrying it into future relationships. Don't go through life carrying enough emotional baggage for a three-week vacation. Lugging around unresolved conflicts, hurts, and bad memories puts your future marriage at a disadvantage before it can begin. Toting this baggage along means that one day your children will take your baggage into their friendships and marriages. Divorce then becomes a vicious cycle, passed down from generation to generation.

Now I don't want to condemn those who have been divorced. Divorce is not the unpardonable sin. No matter how often you have been married, when

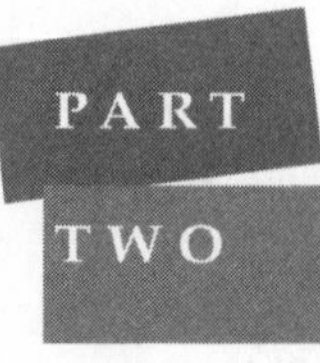

you meet Jesus you get a new start. But divorce should never be an easy way out of difficult tensions. Thousands of marriages have been pulled back from the brink of disaster. Restoring close relationships is always preferable to dissolving them. I've lived through the nightmare of adjusting to divorce as a child, and I've seen how much damage it's done to others who are very close to me.

Marriage is a lifelong commitment, not a weekend fling that we can walk away from when our mood changes. It is far more than a piece of paper. Instead of working to resolve the relationship problems that cause so many divorces, the world's solutions come from casual attitudes toward marriage, as demonstrated by prenuptial agreements. This legal loophole simply creates an escape clause for marriage, an easy invitation to skate away at the first sign of trouble. I compare it to ignoring stop signs: If you do it often enough, I guarantee you'll run into more trouble than you want. Running away from marriage after marriage will drive you into a towering emotional brick wall.

Long-Lasting Rewards

Our older son, Josh, is a stockbroker. That occupation places him in a strategic position to share his faith with people who need to know there is more

to life than money. Our younger son, Jeremy, will soon graduate from college and may enter vocational ministry. He has preached regularly during his studies and sometimes travels with me to share the Gospel. We also have a grandson who we hope will one day accept Christ as his personal Savior and share the Gospel with others.

When I contemplate the rewards of an enduring marriage—a loving wife, a precious family, great in-laws, and wonderful friends—the little problems that have bothered us in the past fade into dim memories. Every marriage experiences trouble. When I lead couples retreats, I say, "If you've never had a fight or disagreement, let me know. I want to come live with you." But allowing minor difficulties to rob me of treasures would have been a serious mistake. If I can't allow God to help me resolve personal difficulties, I won't have much of a message for others.

Remember, anything worth having is worth the work. Too many couples can't see the value of long-term relationships. The day that Debbie and I celebrated our twenty-fifth anniversary will remain in my mind forever. I sang the same song to my wife that I sang on our wedding day, and we rejoiced in the stability our marriage has meant to us and to our family.

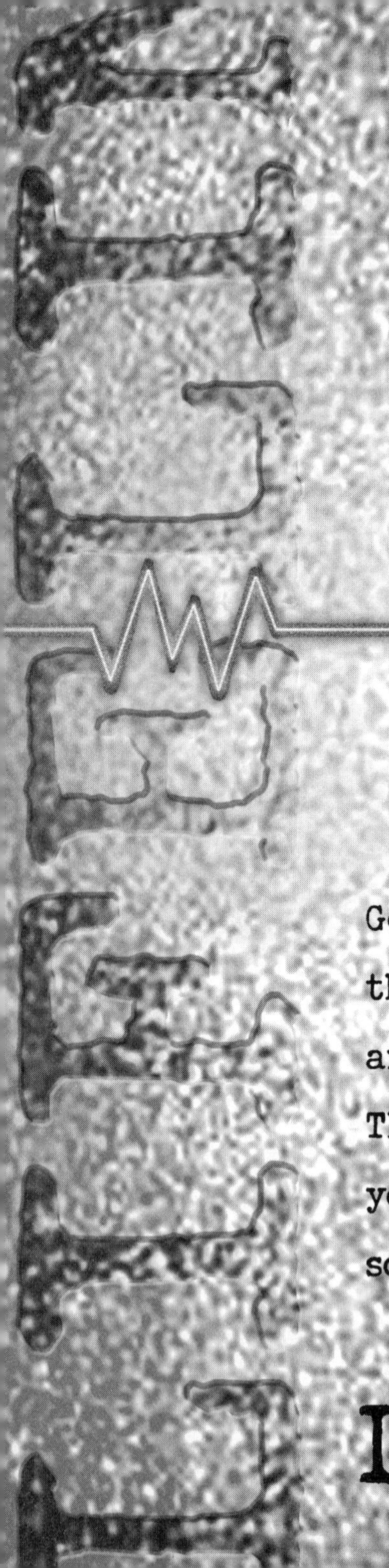

God's a safe-house for the battered, a sanctuary during bad times. The moment you arrive, you relax; you're never sorry you knocked.

—Psalm 9:9–10 *The Message*

LIFELINE

7 The Sting of Rejection

Though he must have stood at least six and a half feet tall, the gangly youth striding to the front of the auditorium looked as if he might shrink into a microscopic ball of nerves. But what grabbed my attention were the chunks missing from his body. Gobs of skin—from a mixture of gaping wounds and sliced tissue—had vanished from his neck, hands, and head.

I'd been invited to deliver a motivational message to the students at this juvenile detention center in Oklahoma. I was used to dealing with troubled young people, but this day tested every ounce of my creativity and resolve. Life had dealt these young people some harsh knocks, and some of

them will struggle for decades to recover from their past.

About seventy-five kids were enrolled at the school. The wires and bars that confined them didn't begin to compare to their emotional prisons. Many of the girls had been raped or molested, as well as some of the boys. Most came from horrible family backgrounds peppered by physical abuse, alcoholism, and violence. This institution offered many the only form of structure and stability they had ever known.

Still, I was curious about this tortured young man. I just had to know what strange gang warfare or sick mind had damaged this gentle giant. Before I could ask, though, he pumped my hand enthusiastically and said, "Thanks. I didn't know anybody knew how I felt."

"What's going on?" I replied.

"I'm here because me and my dad had fist fights. I hate him."

"Why?" I prodded.

He went on to describe a cruel, abusive man who often struck the boy's mother and inflicted verbal punishment on the entire family. The boy took out his frustrations by challenging his father to regular fist fights. His home was a battleground, not a refuge. He longed for peace. The constant denial of

that wish kindled anger inside him until he snapped. One night in a rage, he repeatedly hit his father and nearly killed him. An adult would have gone to jail. As a minor, his alternative wasn't much better.

"But tell me," I said when he finished his sad story, "why do you have all those cuts and scrapes and marks on your body?"

"Well, I deal with my hate by sneaking razor blades from a supply closet and hiding them," he shrugged. "Then, when I get really angry or have a bad day, I go off in a corner somewhere and start cutting my skin. I just slice it a little bit—not deep enough to do a lot of damage. I just cut some of it off."

"But doesn't that hurt?" I said, my eyes widening.

"At first it did," he nodded. "But you know what? That doesn't hurt nearly as bad as not having a real family. I'm used to physical pain. That ain't nothin'. But until you told us about what you went through, I didn't think anyone else would understand the pain in my heart."

"Until you told us about what you went through, I didn't think anyone else would understand the pain in my heart."

He dissolved in tears and collapsed into my arms. As I hugged him, tears welled up in my eyes. I

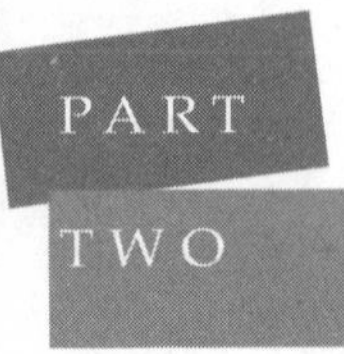

remembered the night I first tried to commit suicide, when one of my stepfathers beat me on the legs until he raised bloody welts. I can remember the smell of beer on his breath as he yelled and swung his belt at me. Then he forced me to take a cold bath so the bruises would sting and teach me a lesson (although I don't know what I was supposed to learn). Rejection certainly played a major role in my childhood.

From the stories I've heard across the nation, I know rejection is a struggle for millions of others—like the two brothers I met in Texas one summer who were bubbling masses of confusion, anger, and resentment. John and Kevin wanted to talk to me so badly they stayed up until midnight, waiting for a chance to unburden themselves. We talked for more than three hours. They had never told their situation to anyone outside their family.

John, the older brother, was especially bitter. He was athletically talented, but his father never came to any of his ball games. To a young boy in the heat of competition, nothing could have been more important than knowing his dad was watching from the sidelines. His father's absence from the games represented what John felt had been his father's lifelong failure to encourage, nurture, and emotionally nourish either of his sons. He blamed

his father for the breakup of his parents' marriage. He felt his dad neglected his mother for so long she finally gave up on him. When his dad remarried and had a child with his second wife, John felt he paid more attention to his new son than to either him or Kevin.

They asked dozens of questions about my family background before their resolve cracked.

"How did you do it?" Kevin asked as his tears began to fall. "How did you forgive your father?"

"Well, it wasn't easy," I said. "It's something I had to choose to do. You have to choose not to be bitter toward your father for whatever happened in the past. Believe me, it's worth it."

"But I hate my dad," John said at one point. "And I hate my mom too."

"Well, you've told me about your dad." I said. "But why do you hate your mom?"

"Because my mom is now a man," he spat, describing how she had undergone a sex-change operation after the divorce. "How can I love my mom, who is now a man married to another woman? How can I love my dad after the way he failed us? If he had paid any attention to us, Mom might not have gone off the deep end."

"Wow. That's not easy to deal with," I agreed, struggling to keep my composure at this new revelation. "But forgiveness is still something you need to work on. Sure, you're angry and hurt. I was too. You have every right to be. But that's not the point. When you hold on to hatred for your dad or your mom, the only person you damage is yourself. Let it out. Admit the anger is there. Then let go of it. I know that sounds strange—our normal human desire is to get even. We want revenge, but that only drives us deeper into despair."

Emotional Struggles

Fortunately, these brothers chose to forget the past. John and Kevin asked their parents' forgiveness and began mending their relationship with them. While not perfect, the brothers have vastly improved since the night they shared their story with me. They were courageous enough to reveal what lay inside their hearts and to face the truth.

When you hold on to hatred for your dad or your mom, the only person you damage is yourself.

That is what helped heal my damaged emotions. The healing didn't happen overnight, just as the embarrassment, humiliation, disappointment, and disgust didn't pile up overnight. It took years of abuse, beatings, and

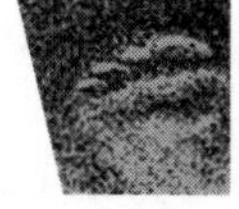

moving from town to town to leave me feeling like a disposable human being.

The rootlessness was one of the worst aspects of my family's life, and Mom's drinking was usually behind each move. Her alcoholism left us continually short of money and on the run from landlords, bill collectors, ex-boyfriends, ex-husbands, and acquaintances who had given her personal loans. On other occasions she was fleeing from bad-check warrants, or the police were looking for her to pay traffic tickets for speeding or reckless driving. Then there were the times we had to move because of the drunken fights that erupted in our home. Upset neighbors would call the police, who either calmed down the participants or hauled them off to jail. Soon after the uproar, our landlord would appear to suggest we find another place to live.

Every day I woke up wondering if this would be the last day in our house or apartment. This aimless existence bred fear, nervousness, and anxiety, which led to drastic mood swings. As I mentioned earlier, I could be happy, sad, and angry—all within a few minutes. These mood swings caused continual outbursts that were hard to control. When my temper flared, I could slice up anyone within striking distance of my tongue.

Moving also meant I had to make new friends constantly, which I dreaded. Besides my shyness and insecurity, Mom always bought us baggy jeans that we had to roll up just to be able to walk. Baggy clothes may be fashionable today, but in the sixties they made you the laughingstock of the neighborhood. I hated my clothes. They made me look like Bozo the Clown, just begging to be mocked.

How I envied the guys who had always lived in the same town! They never seemed to be victims of the cruel jokes aimed at me. I remember the time in fifth grade when a guy jumped me in the hallway and jabbed me twice in the back with a pencil just because I was the new kid in school. While it didn't hurt that badly, the psychological scars of that encounter haunted me for months.

Fortunately, that same year I made some good friends in Florrisant, at the northern tip of metropolitan Saint Louis. I hung around with two guys named Mike. The three of us and a couple of other buddies would go out at night "frog gigging," hunting frogs with our BB guns. We rarely shot anything, though—we were too busy telling jokes, playing games, falling off riverbanks, and getting caked with mud. We delighted in playing practical jokes such as poking a tree limb in a guy's ear just as he was getting ready to pull the trigger and

yelling, "Snake! Snake! Look out, man! It's gonna get ya!"

A couple of these guys also played on my baseball team, which was a refuge for escaping ridicule. I was an accepted member of the squad, and I played decent baseball most of the time. When we weren't practicing or playing in the league, we gathered in someone's backyard for games of wiffleball. Since the yards were too small to use bases, we adapted rules to fit the imaginary diamond. We would play in two-man teams and pretend we were major leaguers from Chicago, Cincinnati, or Saint Louis.

The hometown Cardinals were my favorites, with players like Stan Musial, Lou Brock, Bob Gibson, Ken Boyer, Julio Javier, and Mike Shannon. My hero was Curt Flood, who was faster than greased lightning. I daydreamed about joining the big leagues. I also collected baseball cards whenever I could scrape up enough spare change to buy a pack. But like everything else in my life, they didn't stay around long. I don't know if Mom threw them out or someone stole them, but one day my prized collection disappeared.

While I enjoyed momentary escapes from my dysfunctional family, most of the time I believed nobody cared about me. That made me angry.

Eventually I developed a strange shaking in my hands that resembled alcoholic tremors. I would be in class when my hands would suddenly quiver, making me unable to write. Since I had a reputation as the class clown, my teachers thought it was a game or a show. But all I could do was grab one hand with the other and steady it to avoid further embarrassment.

Gradually depression became my constant companion. I tried to commit suicide again when I was about fifteen. I swallowed a fistful of painkillers, but strangely, nothing happened. I was definitely relaxed, but I didn't have to have my stomach pumped or get violently sick as you might expect from ingesting that many pills.

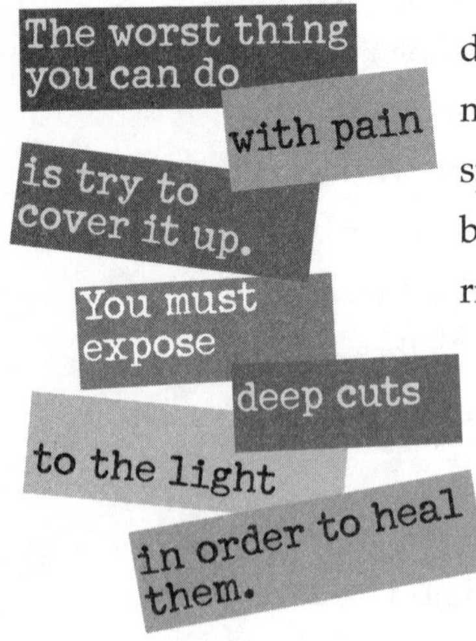

While I can't say I really wanted to die, I routinely thought about killing myself by stepping in front of a speeding car or jumping from a tall building. If you are feeling that way right now, go tell someone about it. You may find you're not alone. The worst thing you can do with pain is try to cover it up. You must expose deep cuts to the light in order to heal them.

Trying to hide how terrible you feel about rejection is what I call a Band-Aid solution. You're kidding yourself and those around you whenever you slap tiny bandages over your heart and make believe the pain has disappeared or when you try to soothe your hurt by sinking into a sea of hatred to muster enough energy to make it through another day. Whatever the problem, it is easy to see the Band-Aid methods that people use to cope. Like that teenager in Oklahoma, some cut themselves with razor blades. Others drink beer or hard liquor. Millions snort cocaine or smoke crack. Many become sexually promiscuous, a pattern that may continue for the rest of their lives.

One of the most painful cases of rejection I ever witnessed involved a girl from Texas named Jessica. As the featured speaker at a summer camp, I was leading a time of sharing and reflection on the week. Jessica walked over, and I put my arm around her to give her a gentle hug. She responded by asking, "Ken, can I go home with you?"

At first I thought she was kidding. The look on her face told me she was absolutely serious. Surprised that she would pose that kind of question in front of dozens of her peers, I said, "Jessica, you've

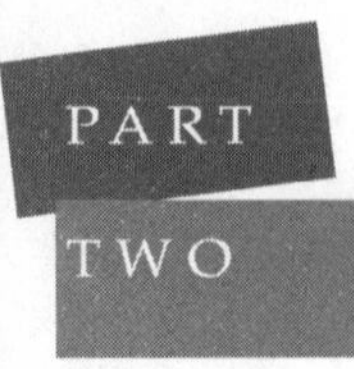

got to go home with your mom and dad. Why would you want to go home with me?"

"I won't be any problem," she promised, evading my question. "I won't cost you any money. I'll clean your house and everything."

"Why don't you want to go home?"

"As of today my mom and dad are officially divorced," she admitted, blinking back tears. "When I left they told me to take whatever I wanted in my suitcase. They said the rest of the stuff would be in the house when I got home but I had to go find another place to live. Neither one of 'em wants me. They said to call my grandparents or whatever."

Sadly, this isn't an isolated incident. On one occasion I spoke over a period of several days at a Christian school in Houston. At the end of the week, a brother and sister came to me. Both grabbed me tightly, but the boy gave me an especially crushing hug. As they did this, they asked, "Would you mind if we pretend?"

"Sure, go ahead," I replied, "but pretend what?"

"We were pretending you were our dad. Our dad has never hugged us. He's too busy for us. He never spends any time with us, and he never tells us he loves us. Just once in a while we wish we had a dad who would hug us."

Then there was Tommy, a young man who

escaped into drugs to deal with his father's rejection. Though a talented actor with professional potential, he couldn't live up to his father's unrealistic expectations that he become an All-American athlete. That, combined with his dad's continual, workaholic-inspired absences, sowed seeds of bitterness and rage. Even after Tommy quit abusing drugs, he couldn't satisfy his father, who made no effort to establish communication or a loving relationship. To fill the gap, Tommy turned to an endless stream of activities, figuring that if he stayed busy enough he wouldn't notice the hurt.

I don't only hear these sad stories while traveling. When our sons were in high school, many of their friends hung out at our house. They regularly came by in the evenings to study or watch videos. On the weekends, some of their girlfriends stopped over too. Some of the guys would spend the night, and many accompanied us when we went out for dinner.

We always made sure we stocked the pantry with snacks and the refrigerator with soft drinks for their visits. I didn't mind feeding my sons' friends, because the atmosphere in our house was the kind I had craved growing up. Nevertheless, wondering why our home seemed to be the neighborhood gathering place, one day I asked my younger son about it.

"I know why, Dad," said Jeremy. "Most of my friends don't like their dads. They don't do anything with them, and they don't like being around them. They like coming to our house because it's cool here."

One of Jeremy's teammates from the basketball and soccer teams who came from a broken home found ours especially attractive. In turn, my heart was drawn to him. When I went to root for my son, I cheered for him too. He struggled with his temper on the field, and whenever that happened I encouraged him to keep his cool. Without consciously intending to, I became a father figure to him. I realized this fact the night I spoke at Jeremy's high-school graduation. Though his friend normally didn't show much affection, he hugged me and whispered, "You were more of a father to me than you'll ever know."

Overcoming Rejection

Earlier I mentioned how facing the truth helped heal my emotions. Rejection is painful, and expressing it often hurts as badly as the injury. There are many other feelings caused by rejection, particularly fear and anxiety about being hurt again if we reach out. Rejection can also produce apprehension that our forgiveness won't be accepted by the one

who hurt us or worry that we are so scarred that we can't love someone else in a normal, healthy manner. Only by facing these powerful emotions can we hope to overcome them.

When I spoke in Texas recently, three different women related how I had helped them face their fears. Each had been sexually molested by a father or close male relative. One said she had been afraid she would never be able to meet the right guy. Another feared she would never find happiness in her marriage. The third wept as she recalled her father molesting her: "I never wanted to face it, never wanted to believe that it happened. But you gave me the strength to call my dad and say, 'I know what happened, but I want you to know I forgive you and I want you to forgive me for hating you.'" Drying her tears, she smiled and told me of her plans to call him that night.

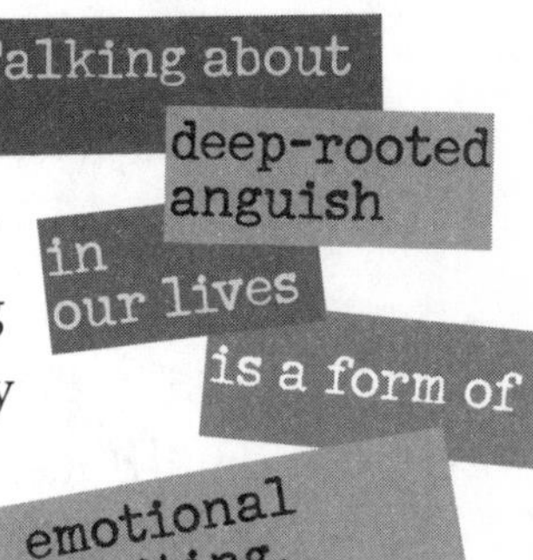

Getting rid of pain and rejection is like throwing up. Nobody likes to do it. Sometimes I'll lie on my bed for hours with my stomach bloated, trying to avoid the steps I know are necessary to rid myself of the pent-up emotions. I try to think happy thoughts or induce warm, fuzzy feelings. But when I finally admit my feelings and cry out to God, I feel 100 percent better. The junk is gone. Cleansed of poison, my system finally has a chance to recover.

Talking about deep-rooted anguish in our lives is a form of emotional vomiting. Holding it back and pretending everything is normal only makes us sicker. When we start talking about it, and the more we talk about it, the better we feel. In the light of day, the secrets don't seem so powerful, nor does the hurt seem so intense.

Confession is good for the soul. So are close friends with whom you can share some of your past and present trials. One of the ways I got over the mound of junk in my life was hanging around with people who had been through similar ordeals. My friend Jeff, who invited me to church the night I became a Christian, had every right to be angry. His father ran off when he was young, and his mother raised him and two brothers. Yet he never talked about hating his father. Jeff told me he had been able to love his father in spite of the fact that he abandoned them and rarely came to visit. He had buried the hatchets. Many others say they have buried their hatchet, but if you look closely, you'll notice the handle sticking out of the ground.

A good family is vital to your recovery. If you don't live in a healthy situation, find someone who

can fill that need. The Graingers taught me what a real family was all about when they took me in at age seventeen. The Graingers weren't perfect, but as I watched them deal positively with setbacks, I realized you can either deal with problems or suffer the consequences of avoiding them. Failing to face the truth means you will carry the same old baggage into your marriage, other relationships, and career. Each will be doomed to failure.

The key to everything, though, is faith in Jesus Christ and his death on the cross. That is the only way I found the strength to forgive my family and get over the past. The Bible says, "Without faith it is impossible to please God" (Hebrews 11:6). People put their faith in all kinds of things, from money to popularity to good habits. These things may give you a temporary boost, but in the end they can't fill you with a sense of purpose and destiny. On the other hand, when I was rescued by the Cross, I discovered the gift that gave me a new outlook on life.

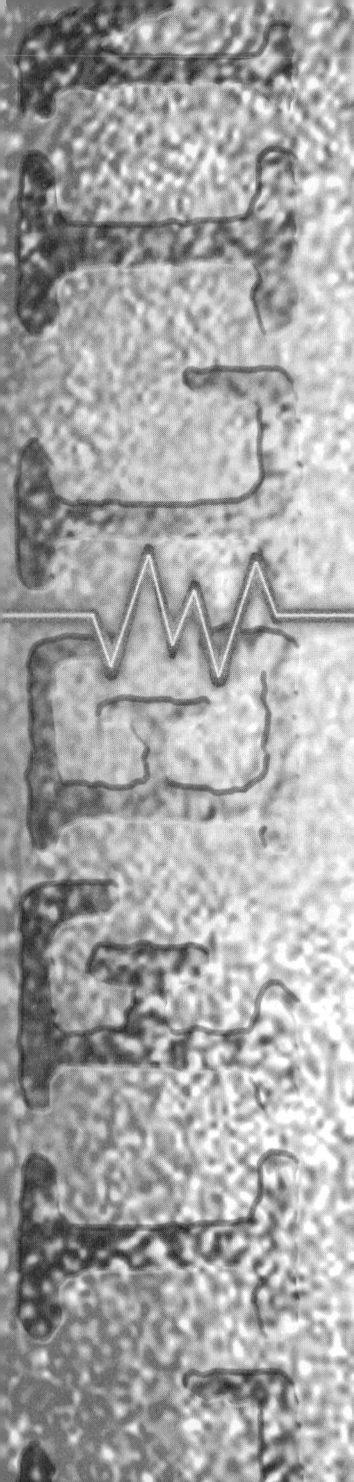

I have been crucified with Christ. My ego is no longer central. It is no longer important that I appear righteous before you or have your good opinion. . . . The life you see me living is not "mine," but is lived by faith in the Son of God, who loved me and gave himself for me. I am not going to go back on that.

—Galatians 2:20 *The Message*

LIFELINE

8 Breaking the Mirror

"Bear." The nickname was appropriate for this massive hulk who stood almost seven feet tall and weighed at least three hundred pounds. Some would envy his size, assuming nobody would mess with a guy that big. But at twenty-one years of age, this shy mountain of a man had never found social acceptance.

Along with his unusual size, Bear was clumsy and never made good grades in school, which attracted plenty of scorn throughout his life. He finally got so sick of ridicule that he started fighting back and hurting others. That may sound great to a macho man, but you can only whip up on so many people before you don't have any friends left. To make matters worse, Bear came from a broken home and lived with his alcoholic mother. When I asked where she was, he mumbled, "Well, she's probably waking up from a drunk, or she's got a hangover, or she's getting drunk." Changing the subject, he then asked me a pointed question: "How do you know God is real?"

"The reason I know God is real is because he's changed my life," I replied. "He's changed my heart, my direction, my emotions. That's all I can tell you, that he changed me."

As if Bear weren't disillusioned and confused enough, he had just recently met his father. For years, his mother claimed his dad had disappeared and nobody knew what had happened to him. Fortunately, his father had become a Christian. He had been praying for his son and invited him to my crusade. But the cruel abuse Bear had endured for so many years had left him bitter and suspicious. After we discussed faith in God, he grumbled, "Everybody's got an angle. The church has an angle. Parents have an angle. Everybody's got an angle. Nothing's real."

"Well, I don't have an angle," I assured him. "I'm just talking to you because I care. I care about your life. You've got to start caring yourself. Let

your dad love you and make up for lost time. I never had a relationship with my dad."

Bear wondered how a loving God could allow so many bad things into his life. I explained that the Lord doesn't *cause* everything that happens. We live in a world that suffers from the effects of humans' bad, self-centered decisions. God loves us so much he gives everyone a free will to decide how we will live, I told him. When people make negative choices, they often hurt others. But that isn't the Lord's doing.

There are a million stories like Bear's, involving those who wonder about the meaning of life and whether they have any reason to go on living. One of the greatest problems created by a dysfunctional background is low self-image. I know what it feels like to hate yourself and slog through a dead-end existence. I understand the heart cry of those who sigh, "It's just not fair."

One of the greatest problems created by a dysfunctional background is low self-image.

Besides the ever-present feelings of rootlessness I felt as a child, I had other strikes against me. In the fourth grade I learned that I needed glasses. It was traumatic enough being the new kid on the block—now I was the new "four-eyes." Some of our greatest insecurities as adults stem from childhood, when physical differences make us objects of ridicule.

To gain acceptance, I became the class clown. I dropped books, threw spit wads at the blackboard, belched loudly, passed gas, and made other funny noises when teachers turned their back to the class. I also tried to win friends by stealing money from my teachers' purses so I could buy ice cream for my classmates.

Some people deal with their low self-image through retaliation. Since someone else made them feel terrible, they strike back to make others feel just as bad. Others search for superficial ways to mask their pain. They think if they can make enough money, their heartaches will go away. Or they try to become popular, mistakenly believing that if a lot of people like them, their wounds will vanish. Still others sink into a sea of apathy, reaching the point where they don't care about anything. Deadening your feelings makes for a very miserable life.

Vast industries are built around changing our physical images. Nose jobs, face-lifts, tummy tucks, breast implants, and liposuction are just a few of the tools we use to reshape our bodies. We want to change our appearance, not only so others will love us, but so we'll love ourselves. One reason so many

women, particularly female athletes, suffer from anorexia and bulimia is they can't stand themselves. Like the young woman I met in Arizona, their obsession with outward appearance starts on the inside.

Amy was five feet, five inches tall and weighed around sixty pounds. A junior in high school, she had a very pretty face but thought she was fat. She tested her body content by pinching a wrist. If there was any loose skin, she convinced herself she weighed too much. To keep her weight low, she took laxatives and forced herself to vomit several times a day.

This young woman lived in another world with a distorted view of reality. One afternoon I visited Amy and her mother in hopes of encouraging them. As we talked and flipped through a photo album, I made a remark about a picture of a gorgeous girl. Amy agreed she was pretty but didn't know her identity. When I turned the picture over, I discovered it was Amy, only three years earlier. She had wasted away so badly she didn't even recognize herself. She finally wound up on the kitchen floor with a can of Drano, ready to drink it in hopes of ending her life. Somehow she managed to call her mother at work and tell her, "Get home, or it's all over."

There is a happy ending to this story. Today Amy

is in her mid-twenties, happily married, and the mother of a healthy baby boy. With Amy, I saw that you don't have to be ugly or abused to have a poor self-image. Lacking certain basics in life, you can feel rejected regardless of your environment.

Fearfully and Wonderfully Made

I believe Christianity is essential to overcoming a rotten self-image—the kind that leaves you feeling so bad you want to break the bathroom mirror every time you look into it. Until I discovered the truth of God's Word, I had no reason to like myself. When my mother held a butcher knife to my throat and declared me worthless, I believed her. I felt useless and bound for nowhere because I didn't know who I was—a treasure created by God. But after learning that God made me in his image, I realized I could live a full life, dream big dreams, and find happiness.

If you don't accept yourself for who you are in God's eyes, you're in big trouble. Jesus told us to love our neighbors as ourselves (Matthew 22:39). But if you can't love yourself, you can never love others. And if you never overcome your lack of self-love, you will carry that problem into all

You don't have to be ugly or abused to have a poor self-image.

your relationships. Plagued by rejection, you will experience conflict with others, you will struggle to set meaningful goals, and you will feel a vague uncertainty about what truly matters.

Psalm 139 is one of the most profound chapters in the Bible. While King David wrote it to praise the Lord, it reads like a love letter from God. Listen to this:

> O Lord, you have searched me
> and you know me.
> You know when I sit and when I rise;
> you perceive my thoughts from afar.
> You discern my going out and my lying down;
> you are familiar with all my ways.
> Before a word is on my tongue
> you know it completely, O Lord. . . .
>
> Where can I go from your Spirit?
> Where can I flee from your presence?
> If I go up to the heavens, you are there;
> if I make my bed in the depths, you are there.
> If I rise on the wings of the dawn,
> if I settle on the far side of the sea,
> even there your hand will guide me,
> your right hand will hold me fast. . . .

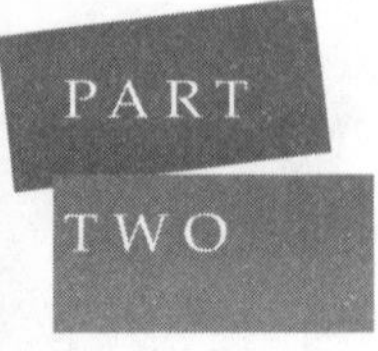

For you created my inmost being;
you knit me together in my mother's womb.
I praise you because I am fearfully and wonderfully made;
your works are wonderful,
I know that full well.
My frame was not hidden from you
when I was made in the secret place.
When I was woven together in the depths of the earth,
your eyes saw my unformed body.
All the days ordained for me
were written in your book
before one of them came to be.
(vv. 1–4, 7–10, 13–16)

There are four truths in this psalm that will revolutionize your life if you will embrace them:

1. God knows us. That means inside and out, upside and down, backward and forward. He knows when we stand up, sit down, lie down, and before we think a thought. With God, we don't need to mask our true selves or worry about our image. He sees right through us and still loves us.

2. God made us. Verse 14 says we are "fearfully and wonderfully made." God formed you when you were still in your mother's womb. He made every single part of you just the way he wanted it. Awesome!

3. God holds us. We can't run away from him, though many try. Although God never forces us to listen, we can't avoid him. Nothing can take us away from him.

4. God leads us. From the very beginning, he had a plan for humans. Even when Adam and Eve stumbled, bringing sin into the world and separating mankind from him, God made a way to resolve the problem. Lost, alone, and messed up, we needed a savior. He sent Jesus to show us perfection and enable us to get to heaven.

The best thing about God's love is that it is available to everyone who accepts Christ, the only way to eternal life. When I became a Christian, I discovered there were lots of people like me. I met others who had lived through similar garbage, yet now they had peace, happiness, and a loving spirit. Each time I asked what had happened, they smiled, "Jesus Christ changed my life." The answer is so simple we can only marvel at why we must endure so much suffering and pain before we're willing to listen.

With God, we don't need to mask our true selves or worry about our image.

Still, when we take that step, change comes. When people discover that God loves them and created them with worth, it changes their outlook. They find a new beginning.

Julie did. The oldest of four sisters from a southern state, she doesn't know her real father. Her mother had been married several times. As a child, one of Julie's stepfathers was an abusive alcoholic who smacked her mother around and occasionally struck his stepdaughters. They all lived in mortal terror of him. Even after he moved out, Julie and her sisters dealt with the emotional hangover of his abuse and her mother's irresponsibility. While they were beautiful young women, their low self-image made them feel like ugly ducklings.

Julie's lack of confidence originated with the absentee father who never cared enough to visit his daughters. Once, right before I visited her town to lead a revival, she told some friends, "My daddy's going to be coming this week." I guess I was the closest thing to a father image she had ever known. But I'm not responsible for turning her around. God did that. One of the most talented singers I have ever heard, she is now married to a minister. Julie's warmth and charm radiate beauty from the inside out. She is living proof that you can make up your mind to change your course and succeed.

Although Dave Busby died a few days before Christmas of 1997, he left behind a long-lasting legacy. Dave enriched my life and thousands of others with the story of how God changed him from an awkward physical wreck into a great communicator. Though doctors expected him to die before his twentieth birthday, he lived to age forty-six. Dave wrote several books and recorded a series of audio cassettes and videotapes that were an inspiration to others.

Dave suffered from a crippling pair of handicaps: Polio forced him to wear stiff leg braces and cystic fibrosis made it difficult for him to breathe. Imagine the mocking that condition would provoke from others and the embarrassment you would feel. Dave grew up as an object of laughter.

After he entered his public-speaking ministry, Dave carried a machine to help him breathe. Sometimes, in the middle of a talk, his bleeding lungs would cause him to cough up red phlegm. "Oh, this is great, Lord," he would exclaim as audiences roared. "This is just great timing!"

One of his most touching stories occurred during his service as a youth pastor. Some teens accompanied him to the airport, where he was picking up a visiting speaker. When the guy walked off the plane, the girls swooned and the boys raved about his physique. A former football player, he stood six feet, four inches tall, with deep blue eyes framing a drop-dead-handsome appearance. Suddenly, the plain-looking, physically challenged Dave became angry. He felt like dashing over and turning the guy's face into pizza. "God, you made a mess," he whined silently. "Look at him and look at me."

That incident could have thrust Dave into a deep depression. Finally, he came to grips with the central issue of his existence: God had made him exactly like he was. Dave could either gripe and moan about it or accept it and let God use him. He chose the latter and set out to change lives. Leaving his position as a youth pastor, he began traveling nationwide. His beautiful wife helped him operate his ministry, and before he died, his daughter traveled with him to share her testimony.

Despite his lack of physical attractiveness, youth flocked to his side, drawn by his ability to laugh at the obstacles life had placed in his path. Though he often chided them for their youthful foolishness and rebellion, they couldn't wait to talk with him. He never apologized for his passion for the Word of

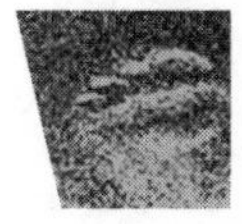

God. People loved Dave because he had a passion for them: He loved others as Jesus did.

I especially appreciated Dave's honesty. He truthfully shared about his weaknesses so that others might learn from his mistakes. One amusing anecdote involved a guy who wanted to take him to the gymnasium for a workout. Though Dave could barely walk, he didn't want to reveal his condition. "I'm too embarrassed, so I know what I'll do," he reasoned. "I'll lie. I'll tell him, 'Hey, I didn't bring any shorts.'" When he did, the man answered, "No problem. I've got some extra ones."

Instead of admitting he was far from athletic, Dave played along. When they reached the fitness center, he went into the locker room and emerged looking like a cross between Pee Wee Herman and Steve Urkel. The shorts he borrowed stretched nearly to his chest. Tucking his shirt inside the shorts, he pulled the athletic socks up to his kneecaps to hide his leg braces. In that moment, he felt far more embarrassed than if he had confessed.

"You know," Dave said, "I would have been much better off if I'd been honest and told him the truth. I could have said, 'Sorry, I can't. You go work out, and we'll meet later.'"

We can laugh at that story. But how many of us

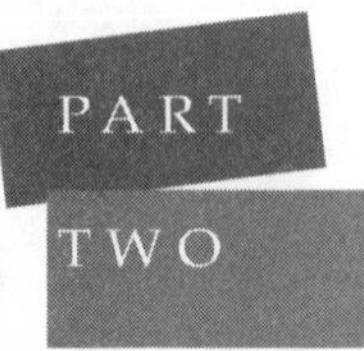

try to hide the truth about ourselves? Most of the kids I meet have a low self-image. This widespread lack of confidence is partially caused by society's preoccupation with appearance. We live in a fitness-fanatic, physically obsessed world. What's one of the first things you notice when you walk into a health club? Walls of mirrors. Everyone wants to gaze into them to see whether their body measures up to the perfect ideal. Channel surf through daytime television, and you can find a dozen fitness shows. (Who would have ever dreamed we'd spend time watching others work out?) It's no wonder I have met so many young women who think they're fat if they can pinch a smidgen of skin anywhere on their arms.

We are bombarded by images every day. If it's not physique, it's the perceived need to wear the latest fashions to look cool to associate with society's upper crust to prove one's value and excellence. If I let such superficial concerns bother me, I would be a basket case. I've got a crooked nose and size thirteen feet, big enough to ski without boots. I was a breech baby, meaning I was born feet-first, making my neck a little crooked. I'm not fond of these things about myself, but I still love what God made. I can't let appearances rule my life, and neither can you if you want a healthy outlook and an

improved self-image. Your value as a person depends on what the Lord says about you, not what other people say.

Fearing the Bogeyman

When you build your self-image on God's Word, your fear will fade. You will lose self-consciousness and operate out of God-consciousness. I used to fret constantly about myself and my performance, wondering what others thought about me and whether I looked good. I compare it to running around looking over your shoulder, wondering if some strange bogeyman is going to leap from the shadows and pulverize you.

Focusing solely on yourself produces worry, fear, doubt, and insecurity. Thankfully, that kind of fear is no longer part of my makeup. I travel forty-five weeks a year, speaking in schools, churches, camps, and other settings. I don't worry about what others think about me. My faith in God gives me confidence because I don't have to depend on myself. Some mistake that for arrogance, but the smile on my face comes from an enjoyment of life. I know who I am. I know that God made

Your value as a person depends on what the Lord says about you, not what other people say.

me. I know that he wants to use me, just like he wants to use everyone who believes in his Son. This isn't happy-talk or a positive-thinking philosophy. My confidence is based on receiving Christ and relying on his strength to break the chains of divorce, abuse, and other negative influences that have diminished me.

It is possible. Many others have triumphed over adversities similar to mine. A man in Louisiana shared with me recently how his parents had been through multiple marriages. His wife also came from a broken home. When they got married, they realized they needed to stop the behavior that had plagued their homes and damaged their youthful self-images. "We realized that religion wasn't going to do it," he said. "We got involved in group Bible studies and being accountable to others. We knew we needed to break the chain of this divorce stuff going on in our families. And so we did."

Leaning on God will bring us success in marriage, personal relationships, and professional endeavors. As the Bible says, "Trust in the Lord with all your heart and lean not on your own understanding; in all your ways acknowledge him, and he will make your paths straight" (Proverbs 3:5–6). I don't mean you will necessarily be rich or famous. Success doesn't come from making more

money and stockpiling more things. True success is knowing peace and enjoying healthy, rewarding relationships in your family, church, workplace, and neighborhood.

The guy who inspired me to get involved in evangelism also came from a messed-up background. Today Don Babin is a pastor in Texarkana, Arkansas, and a happily married father of two boys. But when he was a teenager, Don's youthful insecurities drove him into drugs. Growing up, he wasn't very smart, athletic, or attractive, which meant he didn't fit in with any of the social cliques. He was one of the leftovers—the loners who don't fit in with anyone and frequently gravitate to drugs and antisocial behavior.

This lack of acceptance helped push Don down that road, which caused plenty of conflict at home. He got in fistfights with his father and screaming matches with his mother, often provoked by his outbursts of temper or his latest skirmish with the law. He was in and out of jail as if it were a revolving door. His drug use got so bad he even broke into veterinarians' clinics to steal huge horse needles for shooting heroin.

Don's tragic past only goes to show God's redeeming power. I call Don one of the heroes of the faith. He has provided hope to thousands of young people and adults. Thanks to Don's testimony, many believe that God can use them, no matter how bad the situation looks. Those who knew Don as a teen would never have believed that he could become a college graduate and a successful father, evangelist, and pastor. Because of his faith in the Lord, Don is thriving instead of merely surviving.

Healthy Balance

We must be careful to avoid tipping off balance and allowing our self-image to become the source of puffed-up pride and arrogance. The Bible speaks to this issue: "For it is by grace you have been saved, through faith—and this not from yourselves, it is the gift of God—not by works, so that no one can boast" (Ephesians 2:8–9). God's Word also reminds us that "all-surpassing power is from God and not from us" (2 Corinthians 4:7).

The importance of a healthy self-image lies not only in how it affects us but also in how it affects others. If we have a positive self-image, we can help others to have one. Our good self-image attracts others and inspires them toward a positive self-image. They will feel better about themselves, which, in turn, gives them a desire to help others also.

Conversely, a negative self-image causes you to

lash out and demean others as you seek to drag them down to your level of misery. Those nagged by poor self-images are more likely to live lives characterized by divorce, dishonesty, lying, abuse, cheating, and dysfunctional relationships. A poor self-image is as destructive as a good one is constructive.

A good self-image originates in the Word of God. When you are following biblical truths and obeying God, your standards and morals will be higher. You will be more sensitive to the misbehavior and inconsistencies in your life. Things that you used to consider gray areas will become black and white. What is right and what is wrong won't be so confusing. There will be better balance in your life.

Remember, happiness doesn't come from happenings. If you want to find happiness, you must embrace real life, love, peace, and joy. The Bible says that God is all these things. Joy comes from Jesus. You may not be living in the best of circumstances, but if you have a hold on God and he has a hold on you, life won't tear you down.

God's Word is like a mirror. When I shave in the morning, I don't break the mirror and trim my beard with a sharp fragment. I look in the mirror so I can see clearly to

Happiness doesn't come from happenings.

use my razor and cleanse my face. Too many of you are breaking the mirror, looking at a distorted reflection of yourself, and declaring that you are ugly and worthless. But in the reflection of the Bible, you will see yourself the way God sees you. In God's mirror, you are able to see how to live and come to the knowledge that you are precious in God's sight. Then, instead of wanting to break the mirror when you gaze into it, you will smile at his creation.

PART THREE

and into God's Purpose

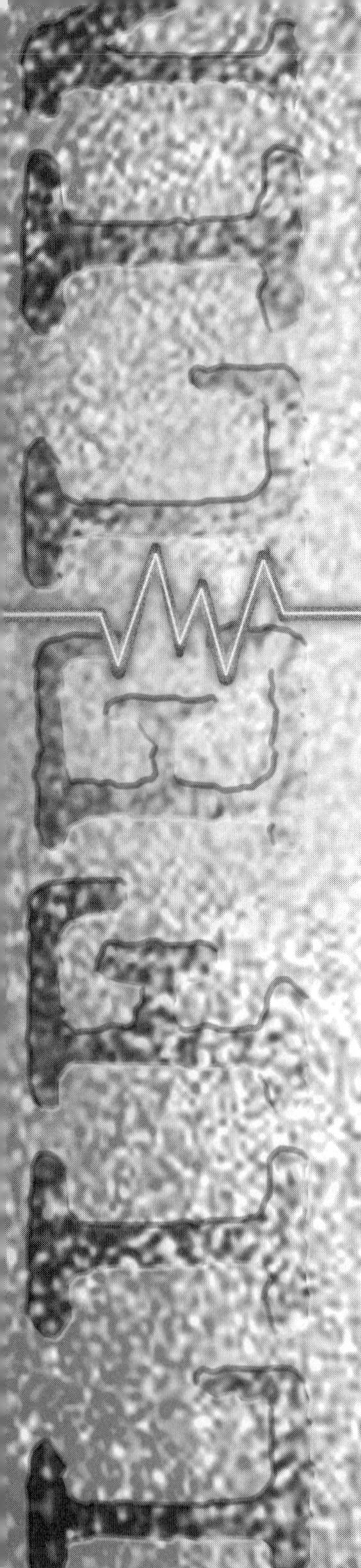

Keep your eyes straight ahead; ignore all sideline distractions. Watch your step, and the road will stretch out smooth before you. Look neither right nor left; leave evil in the dust.

—Proverbs 4:25-27 *The Message*

LIFELINE

NO MORE EXCUSES

Evangelist Billy Sunday once said, "An excuse is a skin of a reason stuffed with a lie." That definition fits modern America, where excuse-makers go to extremes to avoid responsibility for their actions. People never fail. Nothing is ever their fault. Someone else is responsible for all their problems. If it's not their parents, it's the school system, the police, the courts, the judges, their deprived environment, or the rotten referees. This blame game would be comical if it weren't so sad. Excuses have allowed people to literally get away with murder.

Ever hear about the guy in Colorado who accidentally shot his wife—thirty-seven times? Since he didn't use a machine gun, he must have reloaded a few times. But he didn't go to prison for killing her late one night in their backyard. Here's the excuse his attorney gave to the jury that acquitted him: He thought his wife was a raccoon! Or how about the judge in the state of Washington who acquitted a high-school student of murdering a classmate on the grounds he was "morally handicapped."

I thought that story topped them all, until I read about a man charged with first-degree murder for stabbing a bartender to death with two screw-drivers. The defendant wanted the judge to declare the death penalty unconstitutional. The defendant's lawyer reasoned that seeking the death penalty for his client would injure his rights. If he died, the lawyer argued, it would violate his right to freedom of speech.

Timothy McVeigh contends he blew up the federal building in Oklahoma City in 1995, killing 168 people, because of a bad experience in Desert Storm. And so it goes. With so many people looking for ways to avoid responsibility, excuses have become the norm.

Even when they're not deadly, excuses still hurt others. Like the man who walked into a bar one day, got mad at a guy, and beat the fire out of him, breaking his jaw and mangling his eye. Since the incident took place in public, there were plenty of

witnesses. They testified in court, but the guilty party was acquitted because his attorney successfully argued that he had too much sugar that day. (Wouldn't you love to smack someone who irritates you and shrug, "Hey, man, it's not my fault. I had too many candy bars"?) Then there was the guy who wrote more than a million dollars' worth of bad checks. He didn't have to serve any time because doctors claimed he had a disease—he just couldn't add numbers. (Can anyone sympathize with him? I wasn't very good at math either.)

Students have learned from the crazy examples set by our society. While visiting hundreds of schools every year, I hear their endless stream of excuses: They were late to class because their alarm didn't go off; their parents didn't get them up; they forgot they had a doctor's appointment; the dog got sick; the power went out, so they couldn't use their electric toothbrush; or the old standard, "I was sick." (Funny, they weren't too sick to go to the mall that afternoon or the football game that night.) When some kids do something wrong, they mumble, "I'm just a teenager; I didn't know any better." Yet if you tell them they're too young to handle adult responsibilities, those same kids will throw a fit. Others blame their sexual promiscuity or drug abuse on broken homes or abusive parents.

I'm not cold-hearted. I know that growing up in a bad home is a powerfully negative influence. But a dysfunctional family isn't a license to turn around and beat people up, break into houses, abuse drugs, deface property, or mistreat others.

Our prisons are filled to overflowing with men and women whose favorite line is, "It wasn't my fault." I've heard this repeatedly while visiting inmates. When some start excusing their crimes, I'll ask who is to blame. The answers come back, "My parents," "Society," "Racism," "My teachers," or "I didn't have any money." The truth was best summed up by the inmate in Oklahoma who told me, "The best athletes and people with the best abilities are in prison—and they're all there because they didn't want to accept responsibility."

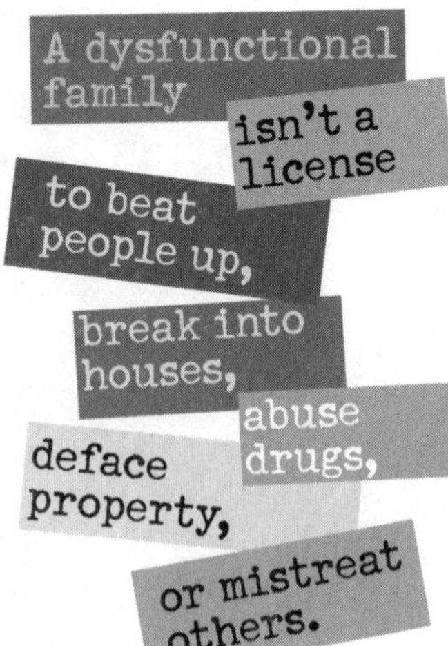

The Beginning of Excuses

Even though excuses have become a refined art form, they are nothing new. To understand their roots, we need to go back to the parents of all excuses: Adam and Eve. Many blame Eve as the one who ate the forbidden fruit in the Garden of Eden and caused all our troubles.

But where was Adam when Eve took that fruit? He was standing right next to her, watching his mate while remaining silent. Countless numbers of men have been evading their responsibilities ever since. Adam and Eve set the pattern, and we have been following it ever since.

Common sense tells us Eve should have been a little leery when a snake started talking to her. I mean, if you walked out to your car and a reptile hissed, "Psst! Hey, pal, come here," what would you do? Talking to the critter was her first mistake. Her second mistake was listening to him. The snake deceived Eve, asking her if God really meant that she and Adam shouldn't eat from the Tree of Knowledge of Good and Evil. That is exactly what the Lord meant, but the devil tricked her by appealing to her pride, vanity, and self-centeredness:

Pride. Satan promised Eve that she could be just like God: " 'You will not surely die,' the serpent said to the woman. 'For God knows that when you eat of it your eyes will be opened, and you will be like God, knowing good and evil' " (Genesis 3:4–5). In other words, the devil lied. He's still lying, making gullible souls think they can become like God or that power, prestige, and money will magically transform them into something better.

Vanity. Eve believed the snake's promises and

acted on them: "When the woman saw that the fruit of the tree was good for food and pleasing to the eye, and also desirable for gaining wisdom, she took some and ate it. She also gave some to her husband, who was with her, and he ate it" (v. 6). Eve liked the way the fruit looked and thought it would make her wise. Satan still uses similar tricks to convince people to try a "quick-fix" remedy for their problems. "Want wisdom? Go to a psychic counselor," he hisses. "Want money? Check out that glittering casino," he beckons. "Want love and fulfillment? Try sex, drugs, and alcohol," the devil whispers.

Self-centeredness. Satan got Eve's eyes off God and onto herself. The fruit she wasn't supposed to eat was from the tree that stood in the middle of the garden. To reach the wrong tree, Eve had to go through all the right ones.

We can learn a lot from our first parents' mistakes, but the point here is to consider how Adam and Eve reacted after they realized they had blown it. They tried to cover up their nakedness with fig leaves (not much of a fashion statement) and hide their blunder from God: "They hid from the Lord God among the trees of the garden. But the Lord God called to the man, 'Where are you?' " (vv. 8–9). Of course, God knew exactly where they were. Just as Adam couldn't hide from God, neither can the

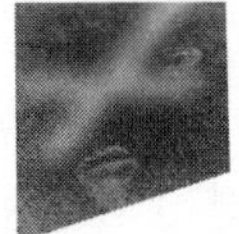

rest of us. Oh, we may try, using drugs, alcohol, hate, bitterness, or bad habits. But sooner or later, God will come looking for us.

When he does, don't offer lame excuses like Adam did. He told the Lord, " 'I heard you in the garden, and I was afraid because I was naked; so I hid.' And [God] said, 'Who told you that you were naked? Have you eaten from the tree that I commanded you not to eat from?' The man said, 'The woman you put here with me—she gave me some fruit from the tree, and I ate it' " (vv. 10–12).

Talk about passing the buck! Adam stood silently beside his wife while she did what he knew they weren't supposed to do. Faced with his own guilt, he instantly pointed the finger at Eve—and, by implication, at God. He was saying, in effect, "Hey, it wasn't me! It was this woman you gave me. She's the one. I was just standing here, Lord, minding my own business, and there she was, playin' footsie with this serpent. That disobedient woman, I knew she'd do something wrong. I didn't want to do it. Besides, God, you're the one who put her here in the first place. After all, I was happy. It was just me and the animals, and we were doing okay. So, hey, you know, it's not really my fault."

Eve doesn't accept responsibility for her actions either: "Then the Lord God said to the woman,

'What is this you have done?' The woman said, 'The serpent deceived me, and I ate' " (Genesis 3:13). Same finger-pointing, same blame-casting, same excuses. Ever watch someone put on a helpless act with sugary-sweet innocence? "Who, *me?* I didn't really understand what I was doing. So-and-so told me it was all right, so I went ahead and did it. I never expected this to happen. I mean, how was I to know something would go wrong?"

It's true that the snake shared major blame—and God condemned him to crawl on his belly and eat dust forever—but Adam and Eve's actions caused a lifetime of pain, conflict, and sorrow for all humans. Their excuses didn't fool God, and neither will yours. Don't go around making excuses for your problems. Racism, rotten politics, crime, abuse, and hatred will exist as long as people live on this earth. None of them is an excuse for irresponsible behavior.

The sad truth about Adam and Eve's story is how their excuse-making affected their children (just like your excuses will one day impact your kids). Their son Cain got mad at his brother Abel and killed him. Hatred and resentment drove him to commit this dark deed. When God asked Cain where his brother was, Cain was ready with an excuse: " 'I don't know,' he replied. 'Am I my brother's keeper?'" (Genesis 4:9). Cain knew exactly where his murdered brother was, but he was imitating his parents.

Excuses remind me of the story about a father who walks into the family room and sees a broken lamp. The cat is swinging helplessly in the air, its tail tied to the ceiling fan. His three sons are sitting there, acting innocent. When the father asks what happened, one boy shrugs, "We were just sitting here praying, and we heard the lamp break. I think the cat jumped on the lamp and then tied himself to the fan. I think we ought to get rid of the cat, Dad. Man, he's bad news."

Wake Up

Satan uses excuses to rock people to sleep. Give some people a convenient excuse, and they'll use it until they die. Take those who skip church on Sundays. "Well, that place is full of hypocrites" (Funny how people will work with hypocrites every day but won't go to church with them) . . . "I don't have anything to wear" . . . "I'd rather play golf and enjoy myself than listen to that lousy preacher" . . . "That preacher talks too loud". . . "That preacher talks too soft" . . . "That preacher talks too much" . . . "It's just not my cup of tea."

Satan uses excuses to rock people to sleep.

Now, I know some churches have problems. But that is no excuse to stay away from every single one. If you don't care for a particular congregation, find another. Don't be like the ex-convict and drug user I met in Arkansas several years ago. Some members at a church where I was leading a revival asked me to visit him. When I knocked at his trailer door, a strange-looking dude with a long beard, greasy black hair, and bloodshot eyes answered. When I invited him to come hear me speak, he asked, "What can that church do for me?"

He related a disappointing story. Several years earlier, this church had been through a vicious split. Before the split happened, he visited on a Wednesday night and found himself in the middle of a nasty business meeting. The members became so belligerent they started swearing in the middle of the discussion. After the meeting broke up, he walked outside and two deacons were duking it out in the parking lot. The only thing he saw that night was hate, he said, and he could find plenty of that at work. "I've never been back," the man said, shaking his head. "Why should I go? What good is a church that makes people behave that way?"

He had a point. Sadly, some will be eternally separated from God because they were disgusted with the way some so-called Christians acted.

Some churches provide unbelievers the ammunition to stay away. These churches claim to be loving, but a closer look shows that they only have conditional acceptance. In other words, "We'll love you . . . if you dress a certain way . . . if your skin is the right color . . . if you don't wear too many earrings . . . if your hair's not too wild." Who can blame the world for being disgusted with church when they hear a message of love but see members getting into knock-'em-down battles over the color of the new carpeting; churches firing their preacher every few years; congregations going through nasty, personality-based splits; or men who stop for a six-pack of beer on the way to teach Sunday school.

Still, citing any of these as a reason to turn your back on God is an excuse. On Judgment Day, you will stand before the Lord, and he will call you to account for your own actions—and no one else's. You can't blame anybody but yourself for your behavior. Others' hypocrisy and failures will be irrelevant.

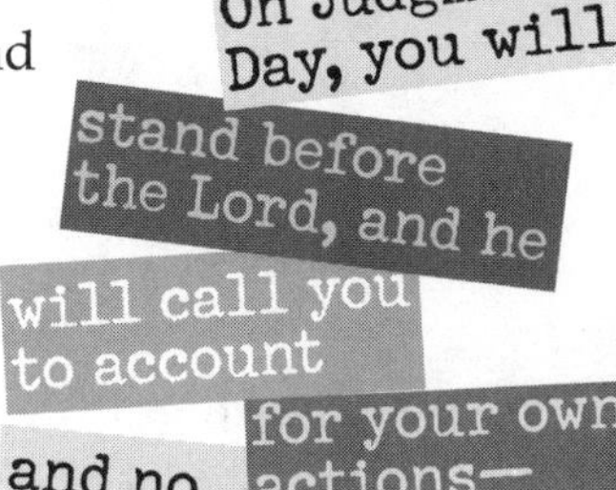

Excuses will land you in the same place as the man I heard about at a meeting in Florida. I had been preaching at a church there for several days. Before my final service,

the drummer in the praise band was lying flat on the stage, praying earnestly. Tears streamed from his face. I walked over and gently asked what was wrong. He told me about a friend from his office who had continually refused his invitations to come to church.

"He was thirty-five years old and overweight," the drummer said. "He came from a bad home and was very hateful. I had invited him to church a hundred times, but he always had an excuse for not coming. Last night you said it could be someone's last invitation, so I decided that after the service I was going to his place as soon as you finished. I knew if he turned his life over to God, the change would be unreal. I was ready to point my finger in his face and say, 'You're going to church tomorrow. If I've got to call the cops and handcuff you, I will. If I've got to put tape on your mouth to make you listen, I'll do that too.'

"So I went over to my friend's apartment. When I drove up, I saw an ambulance at his apartment complex. I never would have dreamed that when I got to my friend's door they would be wheeling him out. He died of a heart attack in his bedroom last night. Ken, my friend's in hell now because he always had a good excuse. But I invited three other friends from my business, and they're all here."

That night, those three friends accepted Christ as their Savior. But it was too late for the man who always had a reason to stay home. Everyone thinks calamity will never happen to him or her. The truth is, you must always be prepared for disaster to strike.

Brenda got ready in the nick of time. In March of 1997, I led a week-long crusade in Texas. A friend kept inviting Brenda, a thirty-seven-year-old single mother, to hear me. Night after night she found a reason to say no until she ran out of excuses. The night she came she accepted Christ. Several days later she led her young son, Joey, to make the same choice. Two months later an F-5 tornado, packing winds over 260 miles per hour, whipped through their town. Brenda and Joey hid in a closet, hoping to survive. Rescue workers later found them dead, their arms wrapped around each other. In heaven, God had his arms around their spirits.

My friend's in hell now because he always had a good excuse.

God Cares

Whatever your situation, don't wallow in excuses to avoid taking the right step. When you make the first move to step out of your past, you might be surprised to discover that you're stepping

into God's purpose. You could wind up like the young woman I met in Texas. By the end of a week of summer camp, I was tired of the food, so a friend and I drove to a restaurant in town. The waitress who took our orders seemed pretty upset. When she brought our meal, I asked what was wrong.

"Well, I've been messing up a lot lately, so this is my last day," she said. "I've been working here for about four years, and all of a sudden I won't have a job."

"Are you a Christian?" I asked.

She immediately burst into tears. When she could talk, she said, "This is weird. You're the second preacher to witness to me today. I talked with one other man, but he told me I'd have to stop doing some things before I could get saved." When I asked, "What kind of things?" she recited some details of her wrecked life. A runaway, she was living with a forty-year-old drug pusher and using drugs and alcohol herself. She also mentioned having an abortion.

"Let me tell you this," I said. "You don't have to stop doing anything. You can ask Christ to come into your heart right now."

"You mean I can give my life to Jesus, and I won't have to stop drinking?"

"Once you become a Christian, you'll want to

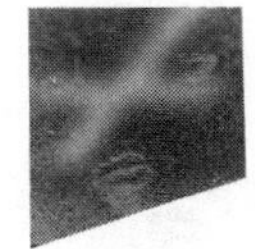

stop," I replied. "I don't know how soon that will be. But he will make changes in your life."

I could see the wheels turning in her mind. Still, she had one more excuse. "Well, I don't think my parents will take me back," she said, shaking her head.

"Well, let's pray about it and see what happens."

After I explained that Christ's death on the cross brings eternal life to everyone who believes in him, she was ready to accept this gift. Less than five minutes later, she called her parents. I could discern their response when she said, "Okay, I'm coming." Next she dialed her live-in boyfriend and said, "I'm not coming home tonight. I'm staying with a friend. I'm coming by tomorrow to get my things, and then I'm going home."

This woman had wanted to escape her screwed-up circumstances for several months, but she kept putting it off, finding excuses to go with the flow. After just one call, she had another chance. Her hesitation came from the same mistake millions make, thinking they have to be perfect before they can change. If you wait that long, you'll be pushing up daisies in the cemetery, still stuck in the same condition.

Another waitress in Texas found help when she stopped making excuses for staying away from

church. She looked so sad the day I visited the restaurant where she worked that I left her a twenty-dollar tip. As I was leaving, she rushed over and said, "Sir, I think you left me too much money."

"No, that's for you," I smiled.

"Well, why would you do that?"

"First of all," I said, "I'm a Christian. And I'm preaching at a nearby church in the morning. Why don't you come?"

Looking at the floor, she said, "You're not going to believe how bad I need this twenty dollars. I'm working two jobs and my live-in boyfriend just walked out. I have a four-year-old daughter. I just didn't think a church would want me. I wanted to go, but my parents have kind of given up on me, and I thought the church had too."

The next day, she came to church and accepted Christ. After I described her situation to the pastor, the congregation responded. Several members bought her clothes and food. One helped her find a new apartment and paid the initial deposits. Had she avoided church any longer, there's no telling where her despair might have led. It is amazing what can happen when you stop making excuses. God is waiting to meet you if you will just look up to him.

Besides, at the heart of the matter, there are no

excuses. The apostle Paul was clear about that when he wrote that the wrath of God is being revealed from heaven against wicked, godless men who suppress the truth about the Lord. "What may be known about God is plain to them," he continues, "because God has made it plain to them. For since the creation of the world God's invisible qualities—his eternal power and divine nature—have been clearly seen, being understood from what has been made, so that men are *without excuse*" (Romans 1:19–20, emphasis added).

ACCOUNTABILITY

God is waiting to meet you if you will just look up to him.

The increasing use of excuses is a symptom of our nation's monumental slide away from God. This habit is so ingrained that it requires intense effort to stop making excuses when everyone else is doing it. The best way to overcome this crutch is accountability. Surround yourself with people who have been through trials and are still here to talk about it. Let them hold you accountable for your actions. Be honest with them about your struggles, and you will see excuses become a thing of the past.

We live in a world that wants instant everything, whether it's instant coffee, instant tea, instant food,

or instant credit. But integrity doesn't come at the snap of your fingers. Being honest and accepting responsibility for your mistakes are traits that emerge over time. Change comes by making right choice after right choice after right choice.

Most of all, cling to the Cross of Christ. Accepting him as your Savior means you will always have an advocate with our heavenly Father. On Judgment Day, Jesus will say, "Please accept him (or her). This person belongs to me." God always accepts us when we stop hiding behind our excuses and let ourselves be rescued by the One who did away with them.

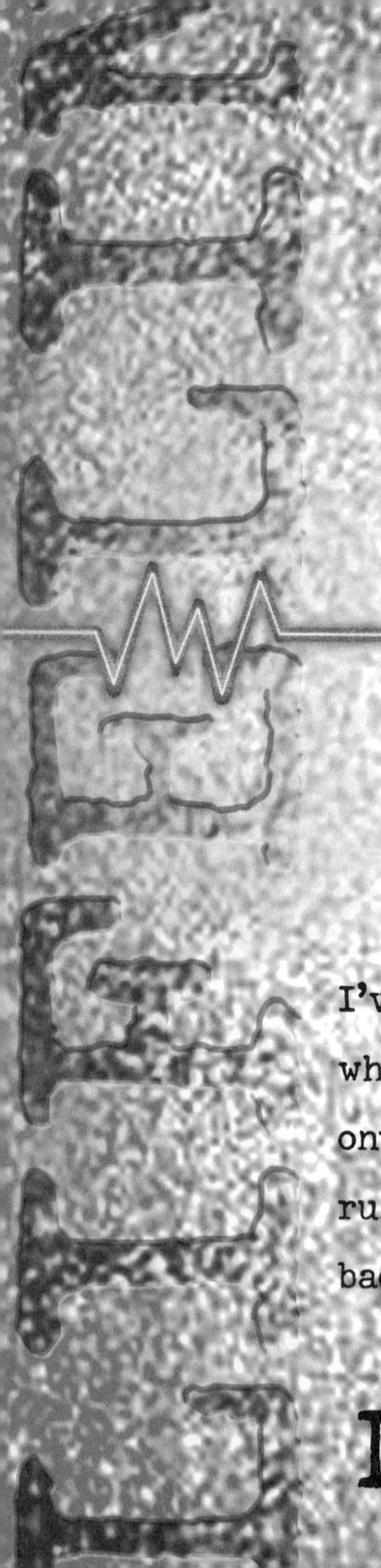

I've got my eye on the goal, where God is beckoning us onward—to Jesus. I'm off and running, and I'm not turning back.

—Philippians 3:14 *The Message*

LIFELINE

10

Move Past Your Past

Refusing to forget our past guarantees our present will be miserable. Dwelling on those negative experiences can rob us of joy, burden us with guilt, dampen our spirits, and hinder our ability to dream of a better future. Satan is the enemy who wants to keep us trapped in illusions. The Devil knows that the person bound by the past will be of little value in the present, so he convinces countless millions to spend their lives trapped in the shackles of their past.

Sadly, in my travels I meet many people who absolutely refuse to let go—such as Andrea, a beautiful woman in her mid-twenties who clings to resentment from her early teens. It began with

anger at her father for neglecting her as a young child. A man's man, he used to be a beer-drinking, chain-smoking, foul-mouthed "good-ol' boy" who spent most of his time at the office or socializing. When he became a Christian, he changed dramatically. Rather than rejoice at his new life, Andrea resented his efforts to become a better parent and spend more time with her. "Why weren't you there when I needed you?" she stewed. "So you've got a new life. So what? Don't you think it's a little late?"

This self-pity fueled rebellion, which led Andrea to try alcohol. Before long she needed a drink every day. Inhibitions lowered, she became sexually promiscuous, which resulted in three children by three different fathers. Liquor ultimately led her into hard drugs and associations with a string of addicts and abusers who nearly destroyed her. One boyfriend shoved a .357 Magnum down her throat and threatened to kill her. Another one broke her nose. One jealous ex-husband paid some buddies to rape her. Andrea struggled with anorexia and bulimia and attempted suicide by slitting her arms and wrists. Even nationally known residential treatment centers weren't able to pull her off this self-destructive path.

Some may shrug, "Well, it's her life; she can wreck it if she wants to." Well, what about the

heartache and expense she caused her parents? Though her father tried to correct his mistakes, some would try to place all the blame on him. But that assumption ignores her failure to accept his apology and move on with life. Her actions have also poisoned her younger sister, who struggles with anger at Andrea and her parents for continually trying to help her.

There may still be hope for Andrea. Her parents haven't given up, and many people are praying for Andrea. Sadly, Becky, also in her mid-twenties, doesn't have that kind of support. When I first met Becky, she was a freshman in high school. A popular cheerleader and softball player, she made straight As in school. Though she hung out with a good crowd and never drank, one night she accepted an invitation to a party. The thirty-two-year-old hostess provided plenty of alcohol. When Becky was half-drunk, the woman helped pin her arms on a bed while six young men gang raped her.

Three months later, Becky tried to hang herself. Six weeks after that, she had an abortion. Unable to cope with her trauma, she dropped out of school and lived on the streets. At night she slept in garages, doorways, alleys, and yards. She was raped again and eventually had two children out of wedlock. While I tried to stay in touch with Becky, she eventually faded away. I don't even know if she's alive. If so, it's likely she is chained to the past.

BREAKING FREE

While horrible victimization may pose enormous obstacles, it doesn't have to enslave you. The past didn't ruin my life, and it shouldn't destroy yours. One of the best examples I know of overcoming the past is Susan, a youth pastor's wife I met at a summer youth camp where I showed a graphic video about abortion called "Hard Truth." This kind of film can send viewers into fits. When people don't like the truth, they will do everything in their power to avoid it or curse it. Some will get enraged and invent excuses to deny its existence.

Susan didn't react angrily at the time, but a year later she called me to describe the video's impact on her life. I cringed listening to her story, which began with her drunken father raping her at the age of ten. During the next five years, he had sex with her several more times and eventually got her pregnant. Soon after she learned she was carrying her father's child, she began dating a young man. They were soon sexually involved, and she convinced him he was the father. They discussed the situation with his mother, who agreed to help pay for an

The past didn't ruin my life, and it shouldn't destroy yours.

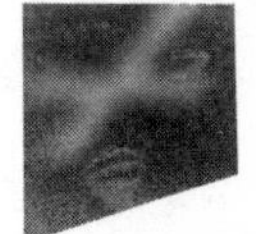

abortion. Although Susan later became a Christian, she hid this dark secret from her former boyfriend and her husband. The video convinced her she had to deal with her past if she was ever going to escape its clutches.

"I've never told anybody," she said. "I've resented my kids. I've resented my husband. I've hated my dad, absolutely hated him. But I've finally dealt with it, and I want you to pray for me."

Susan not only confessed to her husband, she gave a talk to a high-school class at their church and shared the truth with the rest of the staff. She also called the young man to tell him he had not fathered her child and to apologize for lying to him. While Susan wanted to reconcile with her father, his alcoholism prevented that. However, she forgave him in her heart. These steps changed her life. Once a reserved, tough-skinned lady, she became much more loving and open with others. God set her free.

The Lord did the same for Cheryl, a prominent pastor's daughter who struggled with her father's neglect while he devoted most of his time to the demands of a growing church. As a teenager, Cheryl suffered humiliation when several abusive young men tried to take advantage of her sexually. Cheryl was a talented athlete, and several women began showing her attention in college. Confusion

set in: She wondered if her tomboyish looks and her father's failure to show her affection meant God intended her to be a boy. Maybe he had made a mistake. When a lesbian made advances to her, she thought, *I can't get pregnant. Why not try it?*

That touched off a fifteen-year struggle. Though deep inside Cheryl knew homosexuality was wrong, she felt trapped. She accepted Jesus as her Savior during those years, but leaving the homosexual lifestyle—and resolving the pain that formed its roots—was a long, harsh ordeal. About five years ago she returned home, prayed for deliverance, and succeeded in breaking away. She has since shared her story with many women at various conferences.

Though it has a bittersweet ending, another tale of triumph involves Jana, a woman in her mid-twenties. I met her at a youth retreat in Louisiana. Jana was dealing with the pain of a broken home, a mother and a stepfather who drank, and a grandfather who constantly belittled her church activities. Neglected by her father as well, she first drank alcohol to ease her pain, and then she became sexually active. Every year she confessed, "I want to get right with God. I need to repent."

The last time I visited the area, she admitted she hadn't given up her worldly habits. I'll never forget her parting remark: "I don't know what God's going to have to do to get my attention. I know what I'm doing is wrong." A couple of months later I got a late-night call from one of her best friends. While driving home from church in a storm, her car hydroplaned on a puddle. Thrown from the vehicle, Jana landed on her back in a concrete driveway, paralyzing her from the chest down.

While that incident certainly got her attention, Jana's struggles weren't over. She continued to drink and to nurse anger over what had happened. When I visited her in the hospital, Jana admitted, "I know I've got to do something. I can't let my dad and my lack of having a good home, my reputation, all of that, keep me from being what God wants me to be." That resolve finally helped her escape harmful old patterns of behavior.

Jana's paralysis is a haunting reminder of her past, and she is still resolving some issues. Yet she is serving the Lord, using the beautiful voice he gave her to sing his praises and tell others of his love. She also warns teenagers about getting involved in destructive behavior. Because she lost the use of her legs, she never expected to be married. But today she has a

"I don't know what God's going to have to do to get my attention. I know what I'm doing is wrong."

great husband who treats her like a queen. While the past is a reality that can't be denied, Jana doesn't allow it to rule her future.

Mind Games

Those who don't believe in Satan will ridicule me for saying that the devil attacks people and tries to keep them mired in the past. But if the skeptics were honest, they would admit that they, too, have battled insecurities and nagging guilt. They would also admit to hearing voices—not audible ones, but thoughts that bombard their minds and deliver messages as loudly as if they had come through a megaphone. Who do you think puts those ideas in your head?

I know. After turning my life around, it seemed as if every time I did something good, the thoughts came: *You know you don't deserve this. Look at how many people you have hurt. Look at all the nasty things you've done. You don't really think God can forgive you for all that stuff, do you? You ought to be ashamed.* Every time Satan whispered such ideas, I felt unworthy. Not only did I feel guilty about my past, I felt I didn't deserve anything good. In turn, that made me feel guilty for being happy and finally having friends who really cared about me.

At first, I coped by puffing on cigarettes. Smok-

ing three packs a day was a tough habit to break, especially since it provided a form of release. After accepting Jesus as my Savior, I continued to smoke for nearly three years. Finally, the Lord told me, "You're either going to have to let me have it, or you're going to have to live with it."

Becoming a Christian does not mean Satan will no longer attack you; rest assured, Satan will never leave you alone. Faith is a fight, not an easy chair. That is why the Bible commands, "Submit yourselves, then, to God. Resist the devil, and he will flee from you" (James 4:7). We must yield ourselves to God to resist Satan's temptations.

Satan attacks in many ways. Early in my Christian life, I had terrible battles with lust because of the things I saw growing up. I didn't need cable television to watch sexy behavior; there were live shows going on during Mom's drunken parties. Years later Satan still whispered thoughts like, *Who do you think you are to tell your boys they can be pure?*

You must constantly fill your mind with good thoughts and your free time with positive companions. Otherwise, you will open a door for the Enemy, who is always looking for opportunities to drag you down. When you accept Jesus Christ as your Savior, the devil is so angry he will do everything possible to defeat you. If he can't stop you from becoming a Christian, then he wants to turn you into a bad example. He hates God and opposes everyone who calls Jesus "Lord."

This is why the devil spends so much time trying to dredge up your past. It is one of the most effective tools in his arsenal. If he can get you to dwell on your past, you can't serve others; you'll be too occupied with your own problems. My mother used to say I deserved to go to hell. And you know what? She was absolutely right. We all deserve hell. Thanks to God's grace we can choose to escape it and go to heaven instead. Just like we can break free of the past.

Everyone carries around old scars. The secret is to clean them out so they can heal. It reminds me of the time I almost died—literally. During a break at a summer camp, I went jogging on a dirt road. Suddenly a man stepped in front of me. I reached out and caught him with both hands to avoid knocking him down. Then I tumbled awkwardly to the ground, the impact ripping open my right hand. When I got back to my cabin, I washed out the wound, put peroxide on it, and covered it with a bandage.

A week later at another camp, I got violently ill. They put me in the infirmary, where doctors gave me a penicillin shot and blood test as they tried to figure out what was wrong. Next, severe headaches struck. I couldn't sit up or eat. Three days later, I felt well enough to return to camp, but on my way there, I started sweating profusely. As soon as I returned to the infirmary, I passed out. After more treatment, they called Debbie to come get me because I couldn't drive home.

She took me to our doctor the next day. First, he felt the swollen glands in the back of my knees, armpits, legs, and neck. Then, noticing my red, puffy hand, he asked what had happened. When he removed the bandage, he discovered a small stone and dirt still inside the wound. "You've got a touch of gangrene setting in," he said. "If you had waited another twenty-four to forty-eight hours to get treatment, you would have died."

Although the doctor prevented the infection from killing me, it took several shots and three weeks of bed rest for my body to heal. I still have that scar on my hand as a reminder.

The two things people struggle with most are the *past* and *relationships.* If you don't clean up the blemishes of your past and do what you can to

mend broken relationships, they will give the Enemy a chance to wreck your life.

Remember the Good

Despite my mother's shortcomings, she had some positive qualities. When she wasn't drunk, our lives were okay. During those times she was a very clean person and had a sense of humor, which made her pleasant to be with. Occasionally she surprised us with gifts or sightseeing trips. While most of my birthdays were miserable, on those rare occasions when she didn't go off on a binge, I enjoyed some happy celebrations.

You, too, can draw strength by choosing to focus on your good memories. They will provide a security that will never exist as long as you insist on dredging up the pain. One of the best things Mom ever did was allow me to live with the Graingers. Without the influence of the Graingers—my "Jesus parents"—I might not be where I am today. Mom chose to let me go. For all her frailties, she loved me enough to give me a chance to fit in elsewhere.

There is also healing in talking about the junk in your life. Start by telling God how you feel. A woman came up to me after one of my meetings and said, "I'm really mad at God." When I asked her why she didn't talk it over with him, she said,

"I don't want him to know." But he already knows! The Bible says that God knows when we sit, stand up, lie down, or think a thought (see Psalm 139:1–3). If you're angry, tell him. He can handle it. I once heard a woman cuss God out during her prayer. Now, I don't recommend that for your daily devotions, but at least she was honest. You have to learn how to talk to the Lord with the same heart-felt feelings you would express to your best friend. If you're mad, tell him. If you're sad, tell him. When you're hurting, tell him.

You also need to find friends who will help you unburden yourself. I believe the Lord puts people in our lives at specific times to help us over the rough spots. For me, the Graingers were invaluable. So was Don Babin, the friend I told you about in chapter 8. Don encouraged me to share my story publicly. Though Don came from a good home, he wound up involved in heavy drug use that included heroin and countless LSD trips. After becoming a Christian, God answered his prayers, and everyone in his family became a Christian. He greatly influenced me and gave me hope for the future. So did people like Corrie ten Boom, whom I had the pleasure of meeting before her death. Her book, *The Hiding Place,* is essential reading for

If you're angry, tell God. He can handle it.

anyone embittered over past humiliation. Corrie and several family members suffered brutal treatment from the Nazis for hiding Jews during World War II. Yet she forgave them and went on to be an inspiration to the world.

For you, help may come through a guidance counselor, a teacher, a pastor, or a friend. Confide in an older, mature person who will hold you accountable for your actions—preferably someone in the church who has a strong faith in Christ and will be honest. Sometimes the truth hurts. People too often go around looking for pats on the back when they need a verbal whipping. I have good friends who do this for me. If they see me boasting or getting prideful, they quickly bring it to my attention.

However, be careful to avoid dwelling on the past so much that you magnify it into a mountain too tall to climb. Also, avoid going to the other extreme and sinking into a sea of self-pity. When I became a Christian, I wanted others to feel sorry for me and soothe my bruised feelings. When I started going overboard, our youth pastor and a couple of friends would stop me. "Hey, you don't need to keep on feeling sorry for yourself," they cautioned. Finally, God asked, "How long are you going to sit around complaining? You need to get over it."

If the depth of your suffering is so bad that you need to visit a professional counselor, find a Christian counselor who can discuss the spiritual aspects of healing.

Hope and Healing

There is a purpose for your life. The Bible says, " 'For I know the plans I have for you,' declares the Lord, 'plans to prosper you and not to harm you, plans to give you hope and a future' " (Jeremiah 29:11). Although the prophet Jeremiah spoke those words to the Israelites many years ago, the character of God doesn't change, so these words apply to us as well. God has a plan for each of us. He has had a plan from the very beginning. So does Satan. We must decide whose plan we will follow.

Robert Frost's legendary poem "The Road Not Taken" discusses how most prefer to travel the road trampled down by others. Instead of choosing the less-traveled path and overcoming their pain, many would rather revel in their pain, play the blame game, and continue to be paralyzed by the past. I, too, could be a guest on a national talk show and dwell on old wrongs. The difference is that I found healing in Christ. That isn't a popular message. Most people don't want to hear about the Cross of

Jesus Christ, but like it or not, I am living proof that Jesus can heal you.

I saw a sign recently that read, "When you don't see a path, make a good one for someone to follow." Choose that less-traveled road, and you will find hope. You will see that God does have a plan for your life. His ultimate plan was sending his Son to die for us. Some have asked, "What about the children who are sexually abused? What about women who are raped and murdered? Where is the good in that? Why did God let that happen?"

When people choose to ignore God and live like the devil, God isn't at fault. I don't believe God causes everything. After all, he gave us a free will and the right to live however we please. When there's a head-on collision because a guy had too much to drink before he got behind the wheel, it's not God's fault. The blame belongs to the guy who got drunk. However, when tragedy strikes, the Lord can bring good out of the situation, though it may take years to see it unfold.

When people choose to ignore God and live like the devil, God isn't at fault.

The positive role models in my life and the truth of God's Word helped guide me down the correct path. One of my favorite scriptures is Philippians 1:6: "Being confident of this, that [God] who began a good work

in you will carry it on to completion until the day of Christ Jesus." That tells me that although God began working with me years ago, he has more to do. I've been rescued by the Cross. God has called me to step out of my past and into his purpose. But I'm still a construction project in progress, a mess still being turned into a message. God isn't finished with me yet. And if you will allow him, he will also build a brand-new you.

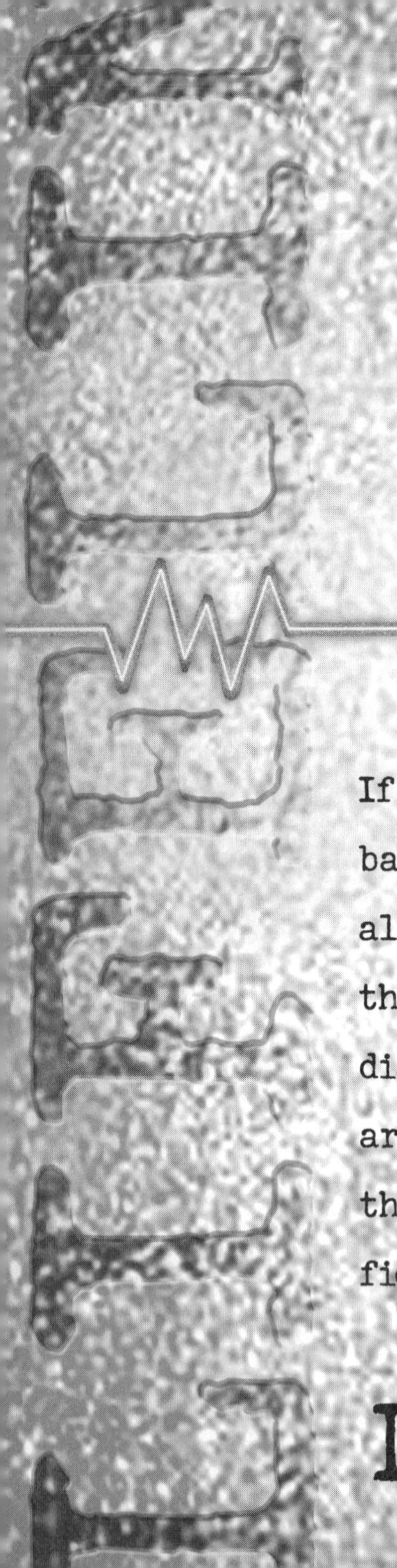

If we give up and turn our backs on all we've learned, all we've been given, all the truth we know, we repudiate Christ's sacrifice and are left on our own to face the Judgment—and a mighty fierce judgment it will be!

—Hebrews 10:26–27 *The Message*

LIFELINE

11 Don't Walk Away

As I was giving advice to the youth in my church, I felt a twinge of sadness. I knew that some of the teens who appeared to be listening attentively would ignore everything I said. After years of service as a music and youth pastor, I was leaving my church to follow God's call to full-time evangelism and motivational speaking. This evening was the last time I would meet with my youth group. I cringed at the thought of losing some of these fresh-faced, bright-eyed young people to society's plagues of drugs, alcohol, sex, and violence.

"Stay involved in a Bible study," I urged, smiling as several heads nodded. "Stay involved with the youth group. There's a couple of cool teachers here.

You need to hang with 'em until the church hires a new youth pastor. Have prayer meetings with each other. Hold each other accountable. You've been accountable to me, but don't stop just because I'm leaving. Check up on each other. Make sure your friends are doing all right. If you don't do these things, you're going to end up in a mess of trouble. You can't do it on your own. You just can't. You've got to have Christian people in your life. You have to go to church consistently. If you do that, you'll make it. If you don't, you won't make it. It's that simple."

Four years later I returned to this small-town church. Sure enough, I met one of the young men from that youth group who had disregarded my advice. Dan's faith had once turned him around, helping him overcome a drug habit and other problems. But after I left he had drifted back into his old ways and suffered the consequences. By age twenty, he had fathered three children. His first child was born out of wedlock. Though he didn't marry the girl, the end of the relationship hurt as badly as a divorce. The next time he got a girl pregnant, he married her. When their second child arrived, the responsibilities strained their pocketbook and their relationship. In addition to his wounded marriage, he had lost two fingers in a work-related accident.

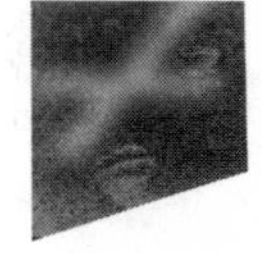

"You know what, Ken?" he said. "I wish I would have listened to you. If I just would have listened, I wouldn't have a baby that I never get to see and two other children. I'm not really happily married. But I'm staying with her because I don't want to go through what I did the first time. If I had just done some of the things you told me to do, I wouldn't be in this mess. Every time I look at my hand, I remember what I've done to my life. If I had been paying attention at work, I wouldn't have cut my fingers off. And if I had been paying attention to my walk with God, I wouldn't have cut my heart in half."

It's been a long time since I talked to Dan, but stories of people straying from God are still common. About a year ago my wife received an urgent message from a youth pastor in Texas. He wanted me to call him back that morning, but I was traveling and was not able to reach him until that night. When we connected, he sadly related his hopes that I could have intervened to prevent a tragedy. Now it was too late.

The previous summer I had led a youth camp where a young woman named Camille accepted Christ. After returning home, Camille got involved in church and shed her bad reputation. But when the school year arrived, she began dating a guy I call Mr. Bad News. Her parents tried to keep her away from him, but like many determined teens, Camille could always find ways around her parents' wishes. Soon she was pregnant. Her boyfriend convinced her to take the easy way out: abortion. The youth pastor had hoped I could talk her out of it. Everyone else had tried and failed. Nearly half the youth group went to her home one night, pleading with her to give birth and place the child up for adoption. On the tragic day, several kids and their pastor followed her to the clinic, where police ordered them to remain across the street. Four hours later she returned home, her problem "solved" by a three hundred dollar payment to an abortionist.

Camille's friends honestly cared for her. They wanted to spare this young woman the agony that now stalks her. This trauma crushed Camille's parents and caused her to withdraw from her peers. The youth pastor has tried to counsel her, but whenever he calls she bursts into tears. She knows what she's done is wrong, but she and her boyfriend didn't have the courage to take responsibility for their actions. I once heard a pastor say it takes a lifetime to find God's will and just a few minutes to walk away from it. Choose your path carefully.

Don't Walk Away

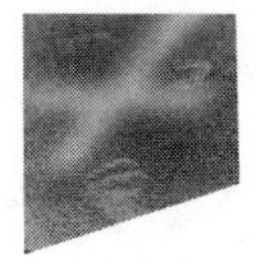

Various studies show that if people aren't Christians when they graduate from high school, the vast majority of them will never accept Christ. Thus, Satan fights hard to distract teenagers with self-centered pleasures and frivolous pursuits. If he can keep people from following God at a young age, the chances of their coming to Christ diminish with each passing year.

If the devil can't prevent someone from becoming a Christian, he settles for the next best thing: backsliding. This term refers to people who slide away from their faith. While it's been a longtime problem, backsliding is getting more serious. In the fifties, nearly 85 percent of the people who joined the church would stick with their commitment. By the seventies, that figure dropped to about 50 percent. Today, pastors say they are fortunate to retain 20 percent of the people who, after publicly expressing a decision to follow Christ, get baptized and become church members. In other words, within the first six to twelve months after salvation, 80 percent of new converts will drop out of church life.

It takes a lifetime to find God's will and just a few minutes to walk away from it.

The risks of walking away from God can have serious consequences. The Graingers had a son who became a Christian as a boy. But he moved away from home when he was twenty and got involved in homosexuality. Seven years later, he returned with the news that he had contracted AIDS. Though he turned back to God, three years later he died, weighing less than eighty pounds and suffering from cancer, pneumonia, and blindness. As a result of wavering in his commitment to God, this young man lost his life.

When I made the commitment to preach, nearly a dozen of my friends made similar commitments at the same time. Today two-thirds of them are divorced, half have fallen away from God, and many suffer from family difficulties and emotional scars. One of my best friends, who sang with me in a Christian band years ago, divorced his wife after twenty-three years of marriage to marry a woman twenty years younger. Most of these men had been involved in some form of ministry, but something distracted them, and they lost their focus. My heart aches for each one of them.

Even when young people decide to follow Christ, they are easily confused. In his book *Generation Next,* demographer George Barna found that 60

percent of American teens claim they have made a personal commitment to Jesus. Yet of these professing Christians, only 60 percent of them believe they will live eternally with God because they have confessed their sins and accepted Christ as Savior.[1] Many are lacking this basic belief of Christianity. Given this weak foundation, it isn't surprising that many Christians later head down the slippery slope of doubt and unbelief. The percentage of professing Christians who attend Sunday school or other spiritual-instruction classes each week drops in half between ages thirteen and sixteen.[2]

Why do so many people who claim to be Christians fail to follow through and live for Christ? I think emotion is a major factor. Some people are easily swept away by an inspirational message or the thrill of joining a large crowd at the altar. Although emotion is often a factor in a genuine conversion, a decision based solely on emotion fades as quickly as the "Amen" at the end of a service.

Another, more serious, cause is the harsh spiritual warfare of our day. When the Graingers invited me to live with them, they invited a girl named Linda too. Linda's struggle was even more difficult than mine because she had been abusing drugs. She endured intense battles with nightmares

and hallucinations and had to resist old friends trying to lure her back to parties.

When people have difficulty leaving drugs behind, they often blame the old friends who continue to offer them drugs. But the old friends are not to blame for their drug use. Temptations will always confront us. In reality, the problem lies within. The Bible says that the devil entices us with our own desires (see James 1:14). Our cravings for a drink, a joint, or a crack-cocaine rush rule our actions. Drug usage among teens has been on the rise again in recent years, leaving more to fight these nasty spirits.

When we come to Christ, it shouldn't be with expectations that life will suddenly be a bed of roses with peace, love, flowers, and sweet music hovering overhead. Nor will it magically be perfect. The same frustrations, weaknesses, relationships, and bills still exist. I remember how shocked I was to give up smoking, drinking, and my favorite drug—hatred—only to discover other headaches. I began to have nightmares rooted in the past. Years later, while leading a youth camp, I burst into tears as I watched a guy hug his mother. Envy and regret sometimes overcome me even when I'm traveling to share the Gospel. Watching families laughing

together makes me long for what I didn't have as a child.

Since you are on this earth, you will have problems. Jesus said, "I have told you these things, so that in me you may have peace. In this world you will have trouble. But take heart! I have overcome the world" (John 16:33). Be encouraged by that promise. It is not when we escape adversity that God is glorified, but when he protects us and helps us walk through trials. As Jesus said to his Father shortly before his death on the cross, "My prayer is not that you take them out of the world but that you protect them from the evil one" (John 17:15).

Driveway of Temptation

What happens to people when they fall? I don't believe they lose their salvation, just as my sons don't stop being my children if they do something wrong. Likewise, sometimes God's children do bad things. When King David messed up and had an affair with Bathsheba, he didn't have to get saved again. He asked the Lord to restore the *joy* of his salvation (see Psalm 51:12). David had lost his joy. The same thing will happen to those who give in to temptation and turn their backs on God. If someone like

Be ready, because temptations will come.

David, who was labeled a "man after God's own heart," can stumble, then none of us is immune. We must always anticipate the Enemy's tricks. I constantly warn audiences to be ready, because the temptations will come.

A good illustration of someone resisting temptation is a young woman in Missouri named Misty, who accepted Christ when she was seventeen. When her older sister brought her to hear me, Misty's life was a mess. After three weeks in a treatment center that cost three thousand dollars a day, she returned to drugs the day they released her. Her sister tried to get her to talk to me, but when I tried to pray for Misty, she bolted from the auditorium.

A month later I returned to that church. Misty slipped in the back door to listen. When I gave an invitation to accept Christ, she broke into tears and stood up. Overcome with joy, people sitting around her wept too. That night I led a service centered on families. Misty returned with her parents and hugged them for the first time in years.

The next summer she attended a camp where I was speaking. Misty brought three friends, and all of them became Christians that week. On the last day I warned everyone that when they got home, the devil would be sitting in their driveway. Sure enough, when Misty got home she saw a car with three old friends parked in her driveway. One invited, "Misty, c'mon. We've got a hotel room and a mess of acid. Let's go have a little fun." She refused to go with them and called me that afternoon. "You were right, Ken," she said. "The devil was sitting in my driveway!" Today Misty is happily married, with a beautiful baby boy and a victorious testimony.

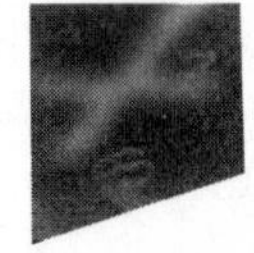

Not everyone succeeds in resisting temptation, particularly those who try to go it alone. Like sixteen-year-old Brandon, who was zealous in his stand for Christ. I warned him, "Whatever you do, don't go back to see your old friends by yourself. Take some Christian guys to help you." Brandon thought he could handle it, though, and went to a party to share his faith in God with his buddies. While he was in the bathroom, they decided to have a little fun. Breaking open a drug capsule, they slipped the powder into his coke. He hadn't done drugs in so long that it shocked his system. His friends thought it would be funny, but that joke cost Brandon his life.

A similar thing happened to another teen in Texas. A loyal member of a Baptist church, Kim was a straight-A student

and valedictorian of her senior class. Concerned about friends who had gone to a hotel to sniff freon to get high, she visited them. Soon the gang was trying to persuade her: "C'mon, Kim, at least try it. Just do it once and see what it's like." When she finally gave in, she died of a heart attack.

Of course, temptations come in many forms. If the Enemy can't lure you back into drugs or other junk, he'll tempt you to give up on your faith. To do so, he employs one of his favorite weapons: fear. People become afraid of rejection from friends or families. I know what that's like. When I accepted Christ, my best friend labeled me a freak and sneered, "I can't believe you're not going to drink anymore." He later cussed me out when scribbling a parting message in my yearbook.

And peer pressure is not a teenage phenomenon—it follows people through their adult lives. Women who come to the Lord often ask me, "What's my husband going to do? What do I tell him when I get home? He won't like this one bit." Others worry, "This sounds pretty tough. Am I going to be able to make it?" The answer is, "Yes, you can." Ever hear the story about the guy who taunted his buddy, "All Jesus is to you is your crutch"? His friend replied, "Well, that's not too bad

when you've been crippled." We all have our own crutches. I can't think of a better one than Christ.

Paying the Price

Another key cause of backsliding is our failure to take our commitments seriously. This can be seen from our skyrocketing divorce rates, disintegrating families, and constant turnover in our workplaces, schools, and churches. Too many people don't count the cost of becoming a Christian. They haven't faced the kind of sacrifice a young woman at our church made.

This Jewish lady's coworker kept telling her about Jesus Christ and inviting her to church. After hearing the Gospel several times, the woman wanted to accept Jesus as her Savior. Still, she attended several counseling sessions before going through with this life-changing decision. A few days before the baptismal service, she told her parents of her plan. They warned that if she went through with it, they would take all her pictures down, remove her name from the family tree, and disinherit her.

As she stood in the baptistery, our pastor commented, "A lot of us don't keep our commitments. We really don't understand how tough it is for some people to give their lives to Christ and what it's going to cost them." Then she shared, "When I'm baptized there will be no turning back from my new life. My parents have said I'm no longer their daughter." Twice she repeated the phrase, "There's no turning back."

Come Home

Each time you walk away from God, it's tougher to come back. And if you keep going long enough, you can reach the point of no return. I'm not saying that God will never take you back, but your heart can get so hardened that you will quit listening. If you've stumbled into a pit of slime, the devil will try to keep you there. He'll whisper, "You've gone too far now," or "You're too bad to get right." But don't believe his lie. You can *always* come home.

A young man in Texas ran away from home a few years ago during his senior year of high school. He drifted around and finally wound up in Wyoming, where a kind family took him into their home. Meanwhile, his parents were sick with worry. They mailed out flyers and called everywhere trying to find him. Finally, the teen decided he would like to go home but was afraid his parents wouldn't take him back. When his

Each time you walk away from God, it's tougher to come back.

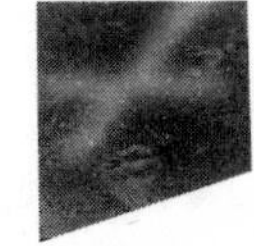

hosts called on his behalf, his parents hopped on a plane and flew to Wyoming. All he had to do was pick up the phone, and his parents came immediately! That's just how God is when we mess up. If you've run away from God, you only have to go to him in prayer, and he will welcome you back. But let me offer three things you can do to keep yourself out of trouble in the first place.

The first and best way to avoid getting involved in the garbage that damages your life is *making up your mind* to avoid it. That may sound simplistic. But the reason some people don't get drunk, do drugs, or have premarital (or extramarital) sex is they decide to abstain before the temptation even arises. Firm decisions will reinforce your stand in times of weakness.

Instead, many people think, *Well, I'll try to stay away from those things*. But *trying* is a sure prescription for *failing*. A college professor made this point with an interesting experiment involving two volunteers. He had them stand in the hallway, then called the first man in and asked him to pick up a beaker of water. "Now I want you to try to drop it," he instructed. The man stared at the water for a while, glanced back at the professor, at the glass, back at the professor, and at the beaker. He studied the container for a while and fidgeted. Finally, after a long, agonizing silence, he dropped the beaker. After it smashed, the professor swept up the mess and told him to take a seat. Calling in the next volunteer, he had him pick up another beaker and said, "Now I want you to drop it." Smash! The man instantly dropped the glass.

The only difference was the word *try*. That one word planted hesitation and uncertainty in the first man's mind, a truth borne out in his struggle to obey the professor. You don't need to try to follow God; you just need to do it. You don't need to try to drop bad habits; you just need to drop them.

A second key to maintaining your Christian walk is *consistency*. It isn't that tough. You didn't have any problems consistently drinking, consistently having sex, and consistently blowing your stack. Now you have to start consistently following good habits instead.

If you attend church faithfully, read your Bible daily, pray constantly, share your faith, and get involved in a youth group or adult Bible study, you will reap the rewards. After all, if a baby drinks milk and eats healthy food, that baby will grow. If you work out several times a week and eat healthy food, you will be in better shape. And if you exercise spiritually, you will be spiritually fit.

Many people go to church once a week but never read their Bible, pray, or do other things to mature in their walk with God. Somehow they think they can grow spiritually through intravenous feedings: "Just stick a little Bible in that needle and let it drip in my veins for an hour. Then I'm gone." That kind of routine will leave you spiritually anemic. Becoming involved in a *church group* is also vital to maintaining your Christian walk. We all need encouragement from others who care about us enough to keep us honest.

Finally, *find your spiritual purpose.* What is your niche? What are your talents? How can God use you? If you find the answers to those questions, you will begin to know the kind of happiness that lasts.

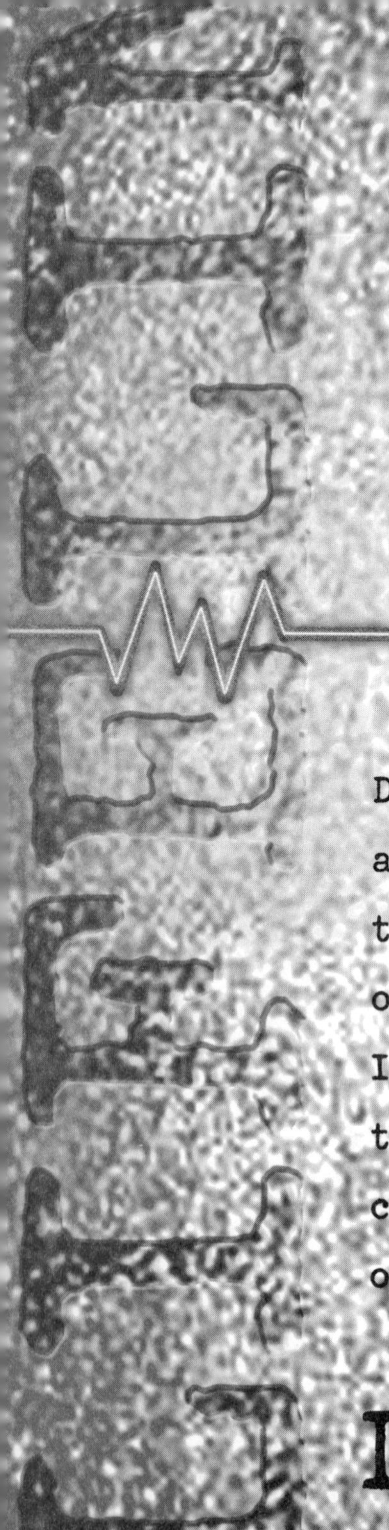

Don't become so well-adjusted to your culture that you fit into it without even thinking. Instead, fix your attention on God. You'll be changed from the inside out.

—Romans 12:2 *The Message*

LIFELINE

12 Renew Your Mind

Slumped behind a slab of glass, the medium-built, gray-haired man wore a depressed countenance. Sam didn't look like a cold-blooded killer. Yet he was awaiting trial for the murder of his wife and a deputy sheriff. As if that weren't bad enough, he appeared ready to follow his victims to the grave. His eyes screamed, "I want to die! I want to die!"

Charged with a pair of gruesome crimes that made him a prime candidate for the death penalty, Sam's future looked bleak. Because he was taking a prescription antidepressant, friends speculated he would squirrel away enough for an overdose. Sam said it himself: "There's no doubt about it," he

nodded when I visited him in jail. "I'm going to die before I even go to trial. I'll kill myself first."

Those who scoff at the idea of mind games should observe their consequences up close. Sam and his wife had battered each other's psyche so often it led to tragedy. Twelve years younger than her husband, Sam's wife was a cocaine addict. Sam loved her and did everything he could to supply her needs. Then he started dipping into it himself. As is often the case when a relationship is centered on drugs, she finally filed for divorce and moved out.

The night before the divorce was finalized, she invited her husband to her home, and they became intimate. The next day she called to tell him he needed to stop by again. Thinking that he would be reunited with his wife, Sam grinned as he rode his motorcycle down the highway. His expression soon turned to rage when he arrived and found her sprawled nude on the couch beside a man half her age who had supplied her with "love" and a strong snort of cocaine. It was her devious way of cutting her husband to the core and letting him know she no longer needed him for anything, including drugs.

Sam wasn't a motorcycle hood or criminal mastermind. He had worked for the same company

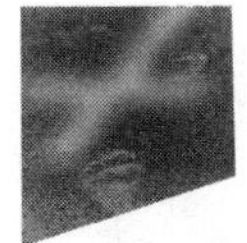

for more than twenty-five years and saved a healthy amount of his middle-class salary. But in one instant, all his worldly achievements swirled down the drain. Overcome by rage, he leaped on the young man, roughed him up, and kicked him out the door. Next, he grabbed his wife, beat her until she collapsed, and dragged her outside by her hair. Grabbing a gun from his motorcycle, he hauled her back inside and flung her on the couch. Gazing up weakly, she mumbled, "I want to die." Sam snapped the trigger.

Meanwhile, the young man he had beaten told an off-duty sheriff's deputy about their brawl. When the officer knocked on the door, Sam flung it open, shot the deputy in the head, and hopped on his motorcycle. Instead of running away, he returned home. Authorities quickly surrounded his house. In the ensuing gun battle, he wounded another deputy before three bullets struck him. He physically survived the ordeal, but in his mind he had already died.

This saga shows the danger of allowing fleshly impulses to control your mind. If you live solely to fulfill your selfish cravings, you will bring home a harvest of lust, anger, fear, shame, and guilt. Sam told me that while still hospitalized from gunshot wounds, he had prayed to receive Christ. But he had not yet been "transformed by the renewing of [his] mind" (Romans 12:2). He dwelt on fear, anguish, and death instead of rebirth, renewal, optimism, and hope.

I don't mean that Sam should be freed from prison. Christian or not, every act we commit carries consequences. Faith doesn't make anyone immune from paying the price. Yet not one of us knows whether we will be alive tomorrow. We need to make an impact on our world by serving God today. Even those in prison have something to do. I can't think of a better place to tell others about Christ. I prayed that Sam would mature in faith before the devil could destroy his life.

Being Transformed

If you are struggling from mind games like the ones Sam suffered from, listen to this good advice:

> So here's what I want you to do, God helping you: Take your everyday, ordinary life—your sleeping, eating, going-to-work, and walking-around life—and place it before God as an offering. Embracing what God does for you is the best thing you can do for him. Don't become so well-adjusted to your culture that you fit into it without

> even thinking. Instead, fix your attention on God. You'll be changed from the inside out. Readily recognize what he wants from you, and quickly respond to it. Unlike the culture around you, always dragging you down to its level of immaturity, God brings the best out of you, develops well-formed maturity in you.

This advice is from *The Message,* a paraphrase of the New Testament. Based on the opening of the twelfth chapter of Romans, this passage contains three primary points:

1. Place your life before God as an offering. When my mother held a knife to my throat and said I would never make it, I felt worthless. But God saw something she didn't. When I yielded my heart, thoughts, and actions to him, he showed me my potential. The Lord rescued a pathetic figure and made something better. Let's face it. I wasn't much, especially compared to the Creator of the universe. Earth is one little dot within his creation, and I stand on a minuscule portion of that dot. Yet when God finished creating everything on the earth, including humans, he said it was very good (see Genesis 1:31).

Still, when I brought my messed-up life to God,

what did I have to offer? A puny body, a confused mind, and limited abilities. The only things I did well were drink, smoke, and curse. Despite my background, God blessed me and gave me a powerful mind, abilities, and faith. In the same way Jesus fed five thousand people with only a few fish and loaves (see Matthew 14:13–21), when we accept Christ, the Lord multiplies us. Ever munch on sunflower seeds? Those little critters grow into good-sized flowers. God can make you strong and tall when he starts with the seed of faith. He wants everything about you so that he can turn you into more than you ever dreamed possible.

2. *Embrace what God does for you.* When our grandson learned to walk, he looked like a real-life cartoon. Stumbling, crawling, and spilling all over the living room, he needed help. When he embraced my index finger, he would scoot across the house so fast I ran to keep up. But as soon as he quit clinging to me, he fell flat on his face again.

None of us is wise enough to make it through this world on our own.

This perfectly illustrates our need for God. None of us is wise enough to make it through this world on our own. We all need God's wisdom, insights, and guidance. God never leaves us. Instead, we walk away from him. We're

like the baby who craves Mommy's nourishment and the reassurance of Daddy's hand and then grows into a rebellious teenager who thinks his parents have suddenly become idiots.

We must be careful about what we embrace. Believing Satan's lies can lead us deeper into deception, pride, cheating, and irresponsible behavior. It starts with just one drink, one fight, or one sexual encounter. Years later we find ourselves making lame excuses for our drug addiction, ferocious temper, alcoholism, sexual immorality, or multiple divorces.

Holding on to God pleases him. In John 15, Jesus uses an illustration in which he calls the Father a gardener, himself the vine, and us the branches. Jesus goes on to say we can do nothing without him. A branch depends on a tree or a vine. If you cut it off, the branch withers and dies. Likewise, when we realize that we can do nothing without God, we can do a lot for him. Our lives draw value, worth, meaning, and purpose when we cling to the Lord.

3. Don't sink into the culture. Many people go through life adapting to the latest fad or hot trend. The only change we should make is becoming more like God. We're supposed to influence others for good, not follow them down the tubes. As the Bible says, "Do not love the world or anything in the world. If anyone loves the world, the love of the Father is not in him. For everything in the world—the cravings of sinful man, the lust of his eyes and the boasting of what he has and does—comes not from the Father but from the world. The world and its desires pass away, but the man who does the will of God lives forever" (1 John 2:15–17).

We live in a misdirected society. The United States is the most materialistic nation in history. Everybody wants to be like the Joneses and will go broke trying to do it. And money isn't the only cultural trap. Look at status symbols such as being "cool." Teenagers would rather die than be labeled a nerd. Some openly display hostility toward authority, like those who flock to Marilyn Manson concerts. Wearing Manson's shirts, walking and talking like him, they imitate his misguided ways. People like this love earrings, tattoos, and whatever fashions will mark them as rebellious.

Instead of being guided by God, most people take their clues from other people. Our culture used to fear God. I don't mean trembling and shaking for fear that God will strike us down at any moment; I mean respect for his awesome nature. When our culture stopped fearing God, we began fearing people. We go to work and wonder if someone will lose their cool and shoot us. Students walk down the halls at school, worried someone may slap or shoot them. We fear tornadoes, fires, what our friends might say to us, or if we will get a job promotion and the money that comes with it. We fear a lot of things, including being mocked if we take a stand for the Lord.

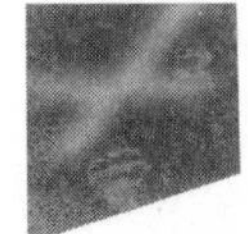

Instead of walking around in fear and being overwhelmed by garbage, Christians should be society's pacesetters. But we still have a long way to go. Last year at an assembly in Texas, I spoke out against marijuana. Afterward four students came to talk to me; two claimed to be Christians. They all wanted to know what was wrong with marijuana. One said, "They use it for cancer and if you have diabetes." Another chimed in, "Hey, I smoke it with my parents. They buy it for me. It doesn't hurt us. What's the big deal? Things have changed. It's going to be legalized."

"Well, let me ask you a question," I replied. "How many of you have cancer? Or diabetes?" As soon as I called their bluff, their heads drooped in shame. "The deal is you're doing it for pleasure," I continued. "There's medical proof that it's not good for your body. Pot smoke has far more tar that will damage your lungs than tobacco. Marijuana is often a gateway to harder drugs. You guys just want to

Christians should be society's pacesetters.

have a good time, and you're refusing to admit what's really going on."

The same principle applies to sex. I meet a lot of Christian young men and women who suppose that heavy petting and sexual foreplay is okay because they aren't having intercourse. But they're overlooking five key issues:

1. They are touching God's property (1 Corinthians 6:20).
2. Their body is the temple of the Holy Spirit, and intimate acts are reserved for marriage (1 Corinthians 6:19).
3. Looking on another lustfully is the same as committing adultery (Matthew 5:28).
4. They should fix their attention on God so he can change them from the inside out (Hebrews 12:2).
5. They should let God bring out the best in them (2 Corinthians 5:17).

In the Sermon on the Mount, Jesus told his disciples, "Be perfect, therefore, as your heavenly Father is perfect" (Matthew 5:48). We can get hung up on the word *perfect,* since none of us can possibly be perfect. But the Greek root of *perfect* means "complete." When we set our minds on God, we

will be complete in him and find the strength to finish the tasks he calls us to do.

The Bible says that renewing our minds enables us to follow God's will (see Romans 12:2). Whenever I mention this truth, many people want to know, "What is God's will?" God's will is not as difficult as we try to make it. God's will is that we look at him, walk with him, and obey him. When we set our minds on him, we will find it easier to make decisions. We will know what to do, when to speak, and when to listen.

Our goal should be to please God, not other humans. Too many follow the pattern outlined by author Ken Davis: "Many people live their lives defensively—just enough work in school to keep from failing, just enough effort at the job to keep from being fired, just enough help at home to keep from being grounded, and just enough faith to keep from going to hell. What a sad way to live."[1] Just getting by is trying to please others instead of offering our best to God. The latter requires meeting a higher standard. But with God by our side, that is possible.

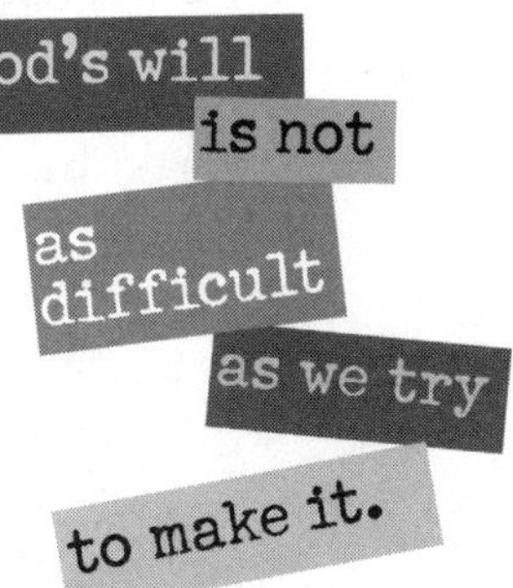

The rapid development of computers and related technologies astounds me. With each passing month, they get faster, store increasing amounts of data, and enable people to do things that used to be science-fiction fantasies. Yet no computer is more amazing than the human mind. While we may not do mechanical calculations with the same speed, humans can absorb, recall, and analyze information in astonishing ways. This is why we must be careful about what we allow into our minds. Years later we can find garbage popping out that we no longer care to remember.

How do you renew your mind? By replacing garbage with wholesome input.

Start with your *music*. While music can be inspiring, Satan loves to misuse it. The devil opposes everything God does, and music is one of his favorite tools of destruction. What would you call songs that praise mainlining heroin, raping women, killing cops, and shooting up the streets? You certainly wouldn't call them *godly*. If you listen to Ozzy Osborne singing about the highway to hell, find some CDs that lift up God and proclaim that Jesus is the answer.

Next, look at your *reading material*. If it consists

of supermarket tabloids, pornographic magazines, and books that stir up violent or negative thoughts, get rid of it. Digest wholesome material about positive people and serving God. Find devotional books that provoke you to meditate on the Lord and dig deeper into the Bible. Recently a guy told me, "Man, I really want a book that's going to slap me, that's going to spank me, that God's going to use to set me straight." I replied, "Well, why don't you read your Bible? God's Word will teach you, discipline you, and turn you around."

Finally, check out your *friends.* If you've been hanging around people who love to cruise the bars, cheat on their mates, speculate endlessly over trivia, and gossip about who's doing what to whom, look for new friends. As much as I liked the guys I ran around with, when I no longer wanted to do drugs or drink, they wanted nothing to do with me. So I started associating with people of great faith. I spent hours talking with them and learning from them. Before long, I suddenly realized I no longer felt depressed.

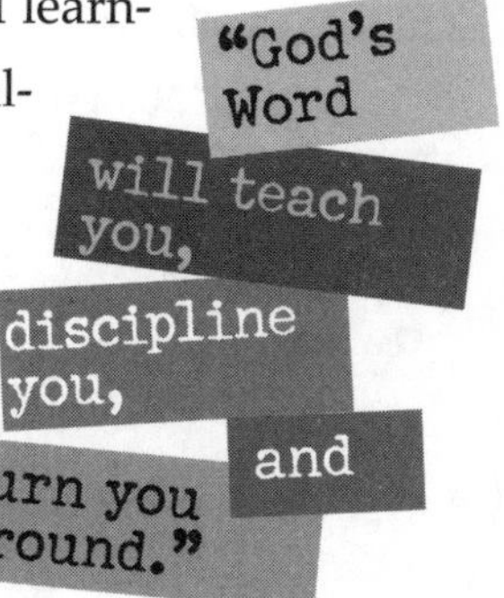

As I mulled over this change, a light bulb clicked in my brain. I could clearly see I had been constantly depressed because I watched depressing television shows, listened to depressing

music, went to depressing movies, and conversed with people who dwelled on the negative, rotten, disturbing elements of life. Is it any wonder this stream of morbid input made me feel sad?

Still, many people are stuck in a rut, sleepwalking through the day with numbed emotions, refusing to change, and making endless excuses about why they can't climb out of the mud. It seems foolish to wallow in the muck, but millions of people do. Why? Here are three reasons:

1. *It's familiar.* They prefer to embrace depression because at least they understand it. They can live a stale existence with expectations of few challenges and no better days ahead.

2. *It's comfortable.* They have been in the mud so long that they've grown accustomed to it. They know from one day to the next what to expect. Many people hate change so much they'll settle for tradition, even when it stinks.

3. *They have plenty of company.* If you wallow in misery, you will always find others who are willing to share your discomfort. Griping and moaning about your sad plight doesn't take much effort. Stepping above the ordinary requires courage.

Now, I realize you can't magically erase every thought of the past. If someone abused, neglected, mistreated, or hated you, you can't just forget about

it. What you can do is stop meditating on it, talking about it, and seething with anger over it. Pain fades with time. When I share my story now, it seems like I'm talking about a little boy I barely know. With each passing year, I find healing—and joy—when I meet others who realize they're not alone. They now know someone else who understands suffering and gives them the hope of putting it behind them.

But we should not necessarily forget where we came from. With God's eyes, we can look at our painful past in a new way. The past can help us remember where God brought us from, making the present sweeter and filling us with gratitude. Rising above the past takes time, faith, and a new environment. If you lived in the gutter for twenty-five years, you won't clean off the grime in a few weeks. Still, you must declare that you're free and live as if you believe it. Take an inmate paroled after twenty years in prison. If he shows up for a job interview wearing handcuffs, he won't get hired. He might as well still be behind bars.

I read once about a missionary who went overseas to a place where people were starving. The natives refused to eat the food sitting right in front of them because they were so accustomed to starvation. Missionaries had to force-feed them to keep them alive. I think many in our nation are starving

for love, life, joy, peace, and freedom. Sometimes Christians must force-feed others with the truth in hopes they will ingest the spiritual nourishment they need for eternal life.

Making It

As a Dallas Cowboys fan, the news during the 1997 football season that Deion Sanders had invited Jesus into his heart thrilled me. Several months later I watched him on a talk show. He shared with the host how he had been a womanizer. At parties, he had indulged in countless opportunities for intimate female contact, which eventually led him to divorce court.

Then Deion made a statement that really caught my attention about how God had renewed his mind and way of thinking: "I lost my marriage because of my thought life," he said. "I need to get my marriage back, and the only way I can do that is by changing the way I think and act." So he was reading the Bible, sharing his faith with others, and trying to help his teammates.

Still, it takes effort to change your attitudes, appetites, and desires. A perfect example is Rebecca, a woman I led to the Lord at summer camp more than eighteen years ago. Although only fourteen at the time, she smuggled in alcohol

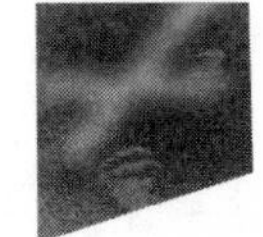

because she couldn't face a day without a drink. Her low self-esteem started at an early age due to a broken home and a father who showed her little attention or affection. She asked Christ into her heart that week but later returned to old habits because of peer and school pressures.

A dozen years later, Rebecca called when I was out of town. She told Debbie that she was at a home for unwed mothers, the consequence of her promiscuous lifestyle. Although pleased she had decided to have the child and place it up for adoption, I was saddened by her inability to follow up on her pledge to live for Christ.

Last year, Rebecca tracked me down to relate the satisfying conclusion to this story. She told me that while she had accepted Christ that summer, she hadn't decided to stick by her decision. "I really believe I got saved, and that's what protected me," she said. "I'm calling to tell you that I'm happily married and going to church. I wanted to tell you that the miserable fourteen-year-old girl you counseled is okay. I went through a lot of garbage, but I made it. I had to come to the point where you led me to Christ. That was the start. I came back to that and said, 'I've got to get it together or I'm going to die.' I finally made it. I just had to make up my mind to do it."

Power Source

Our minds are powerful because God created them. He created what they think, how they work, and what they can do. If we make up our minds to follow God, we will see him do great things. Yet we must be careful to avoid abusing this power and turning our minds into an instrument to manipulate or control others.

When people follow other people, the results can be tragic. Thirty-nine members of the Heaven's Gate cult followed a self-styled messiah to the grave. Dozens died in Waco, Texas, because they turned over their minds to a perverted leader. Hundreds died in the jungles of South America because they yielded their wills to Jim Jones, who mistakenly thought he was God.

The Bible says, "The heart is deceitful above all things and beyond cure. Who can understand it? I the Lord search the heart and examine the mind, to reward a man according to his conduct, according to what his deeds deserve" (Jeremiah 17:9–10). Don't ever give your mind over to another person. Only God can renew it. And when he does, you will be surprised at what he will do.

If we make up our minds to follow God, we will see him do great things.

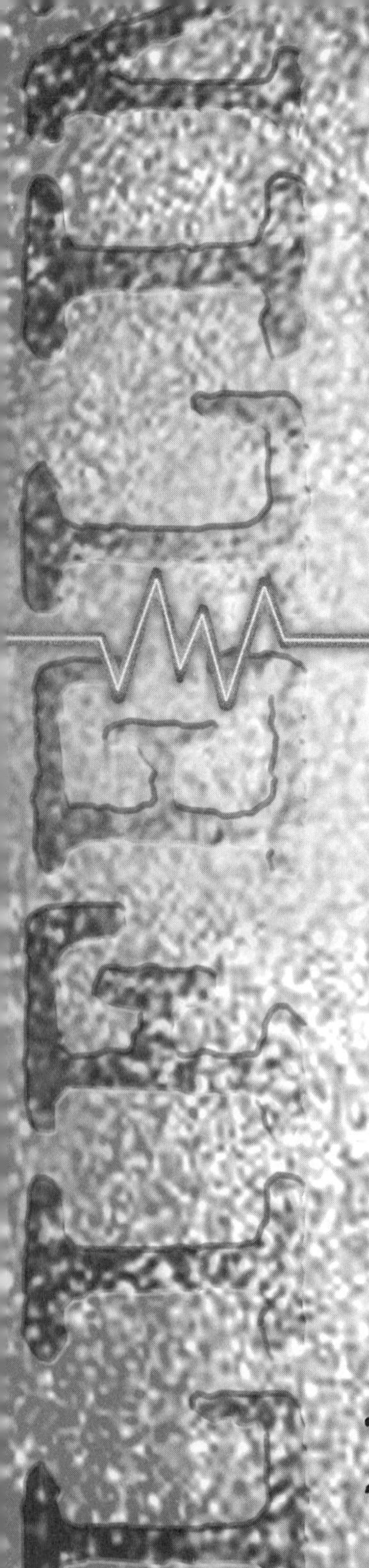

Be prepared. You're up against far more than you can handle on your own. Take . . . every weapon God has issued, so that when it's all over but the shouting you'll still be on your feet.

—Ephesians 6:13 *The Message*

LIFELINE

13

Prepare for Battle

Everyone in Paducah, Kentucky, remembers the day when their small town catapulted into national headlines. On December 1, 1997, a freshman at a nearby rural high school whipped out a pistol and shot eight students, killing three girls.

When I visited the area a couple of years before the shootings, Paducah struck me as another "Mayberry RFD." But during a weekend retreat, I met dozens of hurting teenagers. Of the approximately seventy-five students there, half were dealing with issues too deep for their tender emotional capacities. Several had parents who either were separated or headed for divorce court. Some struggled with alcohol or drug problems. One girl

I counseled battled serious depression because of a date rape, which led her to turn her back on God. And these teens were all members of church youth groups!

This town isn't unique. Our society's lack of personal responsibility and restraint appears in many other ways besides violence. That it occurs as commonly in rural areas as in urban America shows the widespread nature of our social ills. Nowhere is this more apparent than in our nation's schools. What we used to consider a safe haven for children has become one of the most dangerous places they go.

Sadly, Paducah was only one episode in a series of tragic school murders. Whether in rural Kentucky, the plains of Kansas, or the expanse of crowded Southern California, hundreds of students and teachers alike have died at the hands of classmates or crazed intruders. According to the National School Safety Center in Westlake, California, between mid-1992 and December of 1997, 191 students were killed at school, 148 of them dying in shootings.[1]

A few months before the Kentucky disaster, I spoke at two assemblies at a junior high school in Jonesboro, Arkansas. On the surface, the school looked like a clean, modern facility, with the kind of

attractive furnishings I would have loved to have experienced as a youngster. In the gymnasium, a dozen placards advertised conference and regional championships in football, basketball, and tennis. Familiar sponsor names hung from the scoreboard. But what really caught my eye was the sign posted on the front door of the building: "This is a drug-free, gun-free zone." Superimposed behind the letters was a large red circle with a line through drawings of a gun and a syringe. Even with such a stern reminder of the ever-increasing violence in schools, no one could have predicted the tragic shooting in this small town that would snuff out the lives of five people just a few months later.

Fifty years ago, school administrators' primary problems with students were talking in class, running in the halls, throwing spitballs, chewing gum, or being late. Now they have to grapple with the consequences of drugs, alcohol, gangs, violence, dropouts, rape, incest, and suicide. Kids used to play games of hide-and-seek, tag, or trying to avoid getting "cooties." Today many students walk through metal detectors on their way to class. If you doubt that America's teenagers are at risk, consider a summary of what happened in the last twenty-four hours:

- More than 2,700 girls got pregnant.

- More than 1,100 girls had an abortion.
- More than 4,200 teens contracted a sexually transmitted disease.
- About 135,000 teens brought guns or weapons to school, and 3,600 were victims of beatings.
- About 2,200 dropped out of school.
- More than 500 began using drugs, and a thousand started drinking.
- At least 80 were raped.
- About 6 committed suicide.[2]

Everywhere I travel, I encounter human tragedies that put real faces on such statistics, like the young woman I met in the heartland of America in the fall of 1997. She came to hear me preach several times and broke into tears at every service. Finally, she came to talk to me. When she began, "Only my boyfriend and I know this," I could easily guess what she was about to tell me.

A top high-school basketball player in her state, she had already received a college scholarship. But the spring of her junior year, she had gotten pregnant. Three weeks later she'd had an abortion. "We just had sex one time. We used contraceptives, but they didn't work," she said, barely holding back tears. "I'm a good girl. I've never done anything

like that. I'm not into drinking or drugs. I just didn't have time for a baby in my life."

By opting for abortion, this young woman now faces overwhelming guilt. Shame and regret over her actions are tearing her apart. Abortion isn't the kind of serious, life-changing decision that someone who can't legally vote, drink, or sign a contract should be able to make. Advocates of "free love" talk about the right to do whatever they want with their bodies, never about the consequences that follow.

Fairy Tales

When our two sons were small, they loved hearing bedtime stories. As my wife began, "Once upon a time," I would cuddle them in my lap, a poignant moment as I recalled missing this simple pleasure in my childhood. Now we relive this joy with our grandson. Life starts out as a fairy tale, a playground where your most challenging moment is to see how high you can swing. But our grandson will soon leave his fantasies behind. As the years pass, recess ends and life begins.

As the years pass, recess ends and life begins.

Reality isn't always as shocking as three Paducah students' being gunned down in their school lobby. Many young Christians face ridicule and

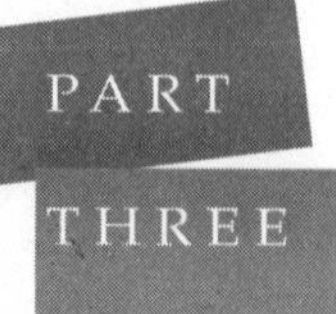

other reprisals for standing up for their faith. In Corpus Christi, Texas, several teens were suspended several years ago for participating in the See You at the Pole prayer gathering. When the movement was fairly new, one girl in Oklahoma was arrested and taken away in handcuffs. Thanks to Congressional legislation guaranteeing the rights of Christians to assemble on campus and the intervention of Christian attorneys, many administrators have backed down. But the harassment hasn't stopped.

At a See You at the Pole rally in Tulsa, Oklahoma, students told me about a group of eighth graders who faced verbal persecution earlier that day. As they sang and then prayed, other students stood behind them, calling them names and mocking their actions.

In Round Rock, Texas, a group of seventh and eighth graders collected signatures on True Love Waits pledge cards, promising to refrain from sexual intercourse before marriage. After placing these cards on display, a group gathered outside for prayer in spite of the stormy weather. As they did, other students made fun of them and continued to ridicule them throughout the school day. When I spoke at a church that evening, one of the mothers of a group member gave me a note about the situa-

tion. She concluded, "I think we should be proud of them and recognize them." The people gave the half-dozen students there a standing ovation.

Before speaking at a school in Arkansas, I encouraged Christian students to invite others to revival services that night. The church was serving free pizza at its youth night—I have never forgotten how the offer of free food first lured me to church. The morning of the revival, I went to the local high school to invite the students to come. After the assembly ended, I went to the cafeteria to eat and mingle with students. One heavyset boy took me seriously and decided to invite some of the popular crowd to hear me that night. When he tapped on the table to get the attention of the football players and cheerleaders, a hush fell over the room.

"You see that guy over there?" he asked, pointing in my direction. "He's speaking tonight. I want to invite you guys to come to church as my guest. We're having free pizza. Would you come hear the rest of his story?" One girl stood up, eyes growing wide and pointing her finger. "Me? Be your guest? Man, you're fat." Then she broke into laughter, touching off echoes of hilarity. That may sound trivial, but not if you were the young man who was simply trying to do the right thing.

However, mocking God—which includes

disobeying his commandments—means one day you will meet your match. That happened to a young man in a small town in Arkansas who accepted Christ in December of 1997 after his lies, drug dealing, burglary, and thievery led him to a dead end. More than once, he had promised to reform, only to end up in another mess a few weeks later. When I visited him, he broke down as he realized how badly he had blown it.

"Dude, as soon as you get out of here, you're gonna have friends who will pounce on you," I warned. "They'll want to get you back for another drink or one more party. The devil's always going to tempt you. The devil *tempts* our faith, but God will *test* it. First Corinthians 10:13 promises God will never give you more than you can handle. There's no temptation you can't resist. When you get out, you better surround yourself with Christian people. Find a youth pastor who will keep you honest, because you're not going to make it on your own."

The devil tempts our faith, but God will test it.

Spiritual Warfare

Some of the best advice you can follow comes from God's Word:

> Finally, be strong in the Lord and in his

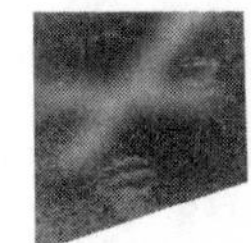

> mighty power. Put on the full armor of God so that you can take your stand against the devil's schemes. For our struggle is not against flesh and blood, but against the rulers, against the authorities, against the powers of this dark world and against the spiritual forces of evil in the heavenly realms. Therefore put on the full armor of God, so that when the day of evil comes, you may be able to stand your ground, and after you have done everything, to stand. . . . In addition to all this, take up the shield of faith, with which you can extinguish all the flaming arrows of the evil one. (Ephesians 6:10–13, 16)

What are the flaming arrows the devil shoots at you? Fear, doubt, insecurity, and lust, to name a few. You will always be in a spiritual battle, especially after becoming a Christian. But with the shield of faith, you can deflect the Enemy's attacks. Faith won't develop on its own, though. To strengthen your faith, you need the daily disciplines of prayer, Bible reading, and Christian fellowship.

Prayer is a solid solution. That was the message a young man shared when he called his parents to tell them he had accepted Christ. "Please don't stop praying for me," he urged. "It works." His parents weren't the only ones who had prayed. The woman who asked me to visit him wept as she described their close friendship. "We've been praying for him, and his girlfriend has been praying for him," she said. "We haven't stopped."

Prayer is the key reason I have seen literally more than a hundred thousand people come to Christ during two decades in ministry. It isn't just my message of overcoming the past. Everywhere I go, faithful Christians prepare the way with prayer. Every time before I speak, I pray that the Holy Spirit will rescue someone else from their messed-up life by the powerful message of the Cross. Consequently, we see families turned around, homes knit back together, and some incorrigible people dramatically changed.

One example of a dramatically changed life is a young man who lives in Arkansas. When I went to his small town in the mid-eighties, Jason owned the toughest, crudest, foulest mouth in the town. He swore loudly in public, a symbol of the lack of respect he had for everybody. He fought constantly and was often hauled off to jail. You name it, he had done it. After a youth pastor described his actions, I went to see Jason. It was the only time he ever dis-

played fear, hiding like a scared jack rabbit. Yet after months of persistence and constant prayer, we reached him. God reversed his direction, and today Jason is a deacon in his church.

At one time, nobody believed that was possible. Just like the three women in Missouri who thought their husbands would never return to church—but they did, and today they are Christians. Another night, a praying father invited his daughter, son, and both of their spouses to hear me speak. All four got saved. They were so excited that they were the last ones to leave the auditorium that night. I constantly see God answering prayers.

As for the benefits of Bible reading, your depth of spirituality will never outrank your knowledge of Scripture. Just like an athlete, you need a game plan and plenty of practice to develop your muscles. Getting into God's Word builds up your spiritual muscles. You learn more about who you are and who he is. I started reading the Bible nearly thirty years ago, and I'm still amazed at how much support the Bible gives me. When I have a problem, God's Word shows me how to resolve it. Here are a few of my favorite verses:

Your depth of spirituality will never outrank your knowledge of Scripture.

Philippians 4:13: "I can do everything through him who gives me strength." That is a

promise. God will give you strength to face obstacles you would never dream of tackling on your own.

Galatians 2:20: "I have been crucified with Christ and I no longer live, but Christ lives in me. The life I live in the body, I live by faith in the Son of God, who loved me and gave himself for me." This verse helps me realize I don't have to rely on myself to survive. God is living within me.

Psalm 40:1–3: "I waited patiently for the Lord; he turned to me and heard my cry. He lifted me out of the slimy pit, out of the mud and mire; he set my feet on a rock and gave me a firm place to stand. He put a new song in my mouth, a hymn of praise to our God. Many will see and fear and put their trust in the Lord." This passage is my testimony. It describes perfectly what God did for me.

Jeremiah 29:11: " 'For I know the plans I have for you,' declares the Lord, 'plans to prosper you and not to harm you, plans to give you hope and a future.' " This verse lets me know that God has a purpose for my life. He has rescued me from something (my past) for something (his purpose).

The other key to faith is Christian fellowship. One of the primary—and sometimes, accurate—criticisms of churches is that they are too cliquish. But cliques exist everywhere, whether at school, at work, or even in large families. Again, you can't let excuses keep you away from God, and God wants us to associate with other believers (see Hebrews 10:24–25). After all, if you want to be a better basketball player, you go to a gym. And if you want to grow as a Christian, you go to a church. Find one that is reaching out to others.

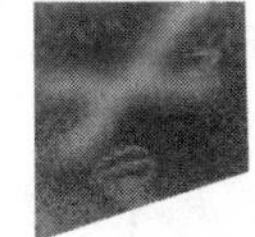

When I became a Christian at age sixteen, I loved our youth group. While some called us a clique, we didn't have any barriers to membership. We welcomed everyone. I drew strength from the love I felt there. I wanted to go there because I wanted to learn and grow in my faith. In church I learned about worship, gained insights from more mature Christians, and enjoyed fellowship that didn't depend on how much money I had or if I had a bottle of booze to share. Sure, you're going to find problems in any church. But remember, you also contribute to the problems.

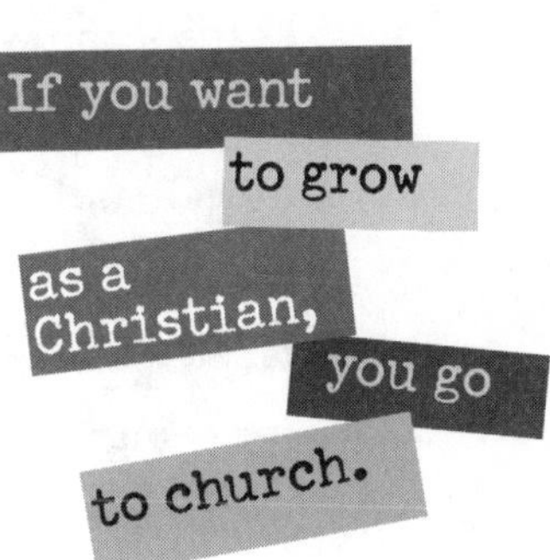

Christian Struggles

Earlier I mentioned some opposition students face. This opposition will continue long after school ends. As long as you're a Christian on this earth, some people will ridicule you, ostracize you, or treat

you like the plague. Friends will ask, "How long is this Jesus thing going to last?" After I graduated from high school, the guys where I worked called me "Preacher Man" and made fun of me. When our older son, Josh, got saved after years of pretending he was a Christian, some of his best friends turned their backs on him. They claimed to follow Christ, but their lives were full of compromise.

Jesus promised that people who genuinely desire to follow him will be persecuted. In the Sermon on the Mount, he said, "Blessed are you when people insult you, persecute you and falsely say all kinds of evil against you because of me. Rejoice and be glad, because great is your reward in heaven, for in the same way they persecuted the prophets who were before you" (Matthew 5:11–12). I see this played out in real life constantly. When Dennis Rodman played for the San Antonio Spurs, he labeled David Robinson a "wimp" and mocked him for being a Christian. Basketball star A. C. Green of the Dallas Mavericks has also faced hostility for his public stands for his faith. You can expect similar treatment whenever you stand for what is right.

Even if you don't encounter public contempt, the devil will attack you. Expect him to play mind games, reminding you of the fun you used to have (leaving out the grief that came with it) or whisper-

ing, "Look at what you did. You used to mock God. You should be ashamed." Remember, your mind is an airport. You must be careful about what you allow to land there. Here's a good formula:

> Sow a thought, and reap an action;
> Sow an action, and reap a habit;
> Sow a habit, and reap a lifestyle.

Mind games are among the toughest obstacles you will ever face. A woman named Lisa learned that lesson after becoming a Christian. For years, her past enslaved her mind. The daughter of a football coach, she became pregnant during high school, right before becoming a Christian. Four days after the birth, she gave the child up for adoption. Yet she couldn't put the past behind her. Whenever she saw little children, self-hatred and resentment burned inside of her. Years later, these emotions hadn't faded away. She came to see me after I spoke in her church.

"I know I'm a Christian, but I just can't get over the guilt," she said.

After we talked awhile, I told her, "You need to come to the point where you love who you are and forgive yourself for what you've done, because God already has."

"I know God has forgiven me, but I haven't forgiven myself," she said, choking back tears. "I just can't get over the pain and hurt."

Though it didn't come easily, she found the strength to forgive herself. She also went to her parents and asked them to forgive her for being angry with them. Though she knew she wasn't ready to be a mother as a teen, she had resented her parents for making her give up her child. Thanks to these steps, she left behind the guilt, resentment, and unforgiveness that had plagued her. It wasn't an overnight process. She worked with an older woman in the church, meeting with her each week for prayer and counseling. Lisa also read the Bible and other books that helped her resolve her feelings. Today she is married, has a healthy baby boy, and boldly shares her testimony in public.

Far more women are willing to be transparent and share their problems than men. Males have a bigger mind game to overcome: pride. They hide their problems behind a tough facade because they're afraid of breaking down or admitting they have any weaknesses. Yet those who 'fess up get cleaned up, like a young man in Mississippi named Mike.

Those who 'fess up get cleaned up.

A student at a Christian college, this six-foot-five hulk is a rough, tough football player. His physical stance parallels

the way he used to live. Mike slept with dozens of women, abused drugs and alcohol, wrecked cars, burglarized homes, and got into plenty of fistfights, including several with his father. His antics caused a couple of colleges to expel him. After becoming a Christian, he re-enrolled in school, where a kind coach took Mike under his wing and began studying the Bible with him.

After I spoke at his school, Mike told me how he hated his father. Although his dad was a Christian, he was so fed up with Mike's past he wouldn't have anything to do with him. Mike couldn't even go home during summer break.

"My dad won't talk to me, and I struggle with that," Mike said. "I hate him. I want to love him. I know I need to do that."

"You need to go call him right now or else write him a letter," I said. "Ask his forgiveness and tell him you love him."

Two weeks later, I called to see how he was doing, and he joyfully recounted calling his father to say, "Dad, I want you to know I love you, and I want you to forgive me for being a lousy son." His father didn't say much, and he hasn't called him back, but Mike has the victory. He can honestly say he loves his father and is confident God will restore their relationship.

Winning the Battle

Jesus told his disciples he came to serve, not to be served. Serving, giving, and being humble are the keys to winning the spiritual battle. At the root of most problems lies some form of desire for self-pleasure, self-glorification, or self-gain. The Bible teaches that in order to get we must give. That doesn't necessarily refer to money. God also wants us to give of our time and abilities to help others. The Creator of the universe took on human form to show us that the way to happiness comes from loving others and putting them ahead of ourselves.

I've already talked about being accountable to others as a way to get rid of excuses and become honest. You also need a determination to reach out and maintain consistency in your life. Those who hold you accountable can help you develop these two habits. One reason for some of the well-publicized falls of televangelists and other public figures during the past decade was their lack of accountability and the fact that they didn't seek to serve; instead, they wanted others to serve them.

Just as we can learn from those who made mistakes, we can try to imitate those who have faithfully followed the Lord. One shining example is Billy Graham, who has dedicated his life to sharing the Gospel and remains humble and honest about his shortcomings.

Coming Revival

Even though the spiritual battle is vigorous and our society seems to be morally declining, I am still hopeful about the future. Why? Because God is sending revival to our nation. Though it seems painfully slow at times, the signs are unmistakable. Over the years, the numbers of conversions at my meetings have steadily increased. Satan is being defeated, and Christians are emerging triumphant from the battle.

I am seeing more adults than ever come to God. Most people who become Christians reach that decision in their youth. With each passing year, the hearts of those who refuse to accept God continue to harden. Seeing increasing numbers of older folks at the altar is a sure sign that the Holy Spirit is performing miracles. Millions of people are looking for the truth. They want something more than a song and a church program. They're looking for authentic love, peace, and hope—which can only be found in a personal relationship with Christ.

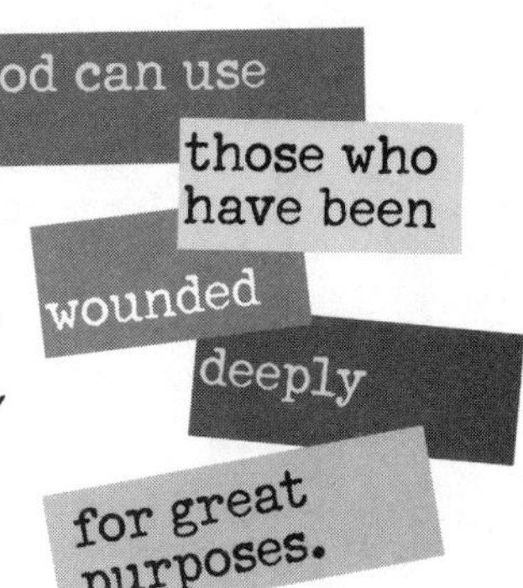

As long as Jesus is alive, there will always be hope. No matter how bad things may appear today, tomorrow can be better. I am living proof that God can use those who have been wounded deeply for great purposes. What the devil has used in an attempt to destroy you, the Lord can transform into something good. When you are rescued by the One who died on the cross for you, you will be able to step out of your past and into God's purpose of healing and hope.

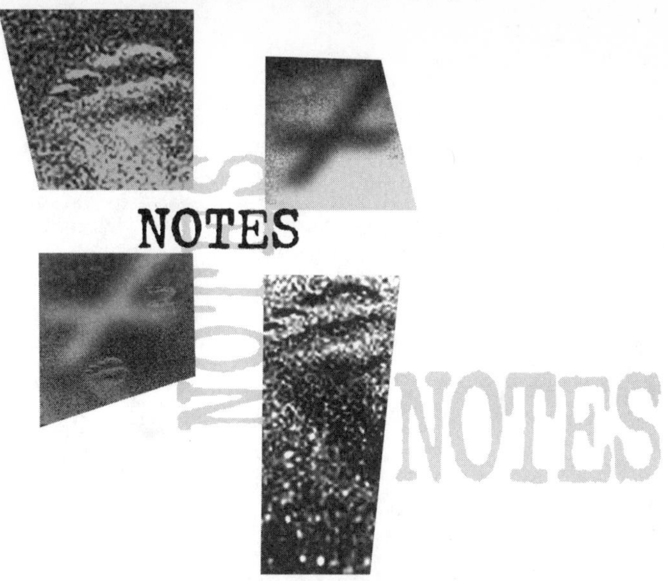

Chapter One. Butchered Dreams

1. Madeline Nash, "Addicted," *Time*, 5 May 1997.

2. "Depression, drinking costs will pass cancer by 2010, experts say," from an Associated Press report, 12 December 1997.

Chapter Two. Broken Homes

1. David Blankenhorn, *Fatherless America* (New York: Basic Books, 1995), 1.

2. Kevin Miller, "Ending the Church's Silence on Divorce," *Christianity Today*, 17 November 1997, 52.

3. Blankenhorn, *Fatherless America.*

Chapter Five. LSD (Lies, Sex, and Death)

1. Gail Epstein and Frances Robles, "Forbidden to date," *Miami Herald*, 27 November, 1995, 1.

2. Margaret A. Fischl, et. al., "Heterosexual Transmission of Human Immunodeficiency Virus (HIV); Relationship of Sexual Practices to Seroconversion," Third International Conference on AIDS, June 1987, *Abstracts Volume*, 178.

3. "Alcohol problems more likely for young drinkers, report shows," from *Baptist Press* news service, 16 January 1998.

Chapter Six. Home Wreckers

1. Francis Frangipane, *The Three Battlegrounds* (Cedar Rapids, Iowa: Arrow Publishing, 1989), 25.

Chapter Eleven. Don't Walk Away

1. George Barna, *Generation Next,* (Ventura, Calif.: Regal Books, 1995), 77–78.

2. Ibid., 88.

Chapter Twelve. Renew Your Mind

1. Ken Davis, "How to Live with Your Parents," from *True Love Waits Bible,* (Nashville, Tenn.: Broadman & Holman Publishers, 1996), xv.

Chapter Thirteen. Prepare for Battle

1. Art Toalston, "We cannot run away from public schools after shootings," *Baptist Press* news service, 3 December 1997.

2. Josh McDowell, *Right from Wrong* (Dallas: Word Publishing, 1994), 6.